MIRACLES
in Tough Times

WHEN MIRACLES HAPPEN
True Stories of God's Divine Touch

Edited by Mary Hollingsworth

Guideposts
New York, New York

Acknowledgments

Every attempt has been made to credit the sources of copyrighted material used in this book. If any such acknowledgment has been inadvertently omitted or miscredited, receipt of such information would be appreciated.

All material that originally appeared in Guideposts publications is reprinted with permission. Copyright © by Guideposts.

Unless otherwise noted, Scripture quotations are from the New Century Version®. Copyright © 1987, 1988, 1991 by Thomas Nelson, Inc. All rights reserved.

Quotations designated NIV are from the Holy Bible, New International Version. Copyright © 1973, 1978, 1984, International Bible Society. Used by permission of Zondervan Bible Publishers.

Quotations designated TLB are from the *Living Bible* copyright © 1971 by Tyndale House Publishers, Wheaton, Ill. Used by permission.

"It All Depends on How You Look at It," "A Bushel and a Peck," and "Thinking with the Heart" published by permission from *Whispers from Heaven*, copyright © 2002, 2003 Publications International, Ltd.

"An Angel's Visit" by Nancy B. Gibbs, "Drive-By Blessing" by Susy Flory, "A Teacher's Nightmare" written by BJ Taylor, "Reach Out and Touch Someone," "The Hardest Prayer I Ever Prayed," and "Through Eyes That Could Not See" by Marcia K. Leaser, "Chicken Dumpling Soup, Turtles, and a Miracle" by Pamela Kessler, "A Dilemma—To Go Home or Not" written by Betty Beaver Cantwell, "An Unexpected Miracle," and "More Than Football" written by Greg Asimakoupoulos, "Silent Faith," and "Chemo Hair" by Susan Farr Fahncke, "The Truth about Fairy Tales" by Nancy Jo Eckerson, "Grocery Cart Angel" by Susan Sundwall, "To Live Again" by Nanette Thorsen-Snipes, "The Sparrow at Starbuck's" by John Thomas Oaks www.johnthomasoaks.com, "In His Perfect Time" by Carla M. Zwahlen, "Bill's Strength" by Cheryl Abbott, "The Stolen Car" by Donna Collins Tinsley, "All She Had Was Faith and Five Dollars" written by Elizabeth Blake, "The Music Still Plays" by Rebecca Barlow Jordan, and "Waiting at the Window" by Paula Hemingway; are used by permission of the authors.

Editorial, research, and content development managed by Shady Oaks Studio, Bedford, Texas. Team members: Patty Crowley, Rhonda Hogan, Mary Hollingsworth, Mary Kay Knox, Kathryn Murray, Nancy Sullivan, Stephanie Terry, and Barbara Tork.

www.guideposts.org
(800) 431-2344
Guideposts Books & Inspirational Media Division
Illustrations by Ron Bucalo
Jacket design and photo by The DesignWorks Group, Inc.

Printed in the United States of America

Contents

𝒞HAPTER 2 SEARCHING FOR HOPE

𝒞HAPTER 3 KEEPING THE FAITH

*C*HAPTER 4   WAITING FOR THE SUNRISE

CHAPTER 5   DREAMING OF TOMORROW

Introduction

W hen it rains, it pours!" says the old Morton
Salt ad. And life is like that, too, isn't it?
When tough times come, as they inevitably will, often
they come with a vengeance—trouble upon trouble,
heartache upon heartache, loss upon loss. And we feel
overwhelmed by them, crushed under the weight of dif-
ficulties and cares. Hopeless.

Fortunately, tough times don't usually last, but tough
people do. And while battling the storms of life is never
easy, we tend to pull our coat collars up around our ears
and walk into the wind, determined to get through it.
Eventually, we emerge on the other side. Wiser now.
Perhaps bruised and broken. Smile a little crooked and
more forced. Eyes not quite as shining as before. A little
dirty and scuffed up. But alive. We survived!

Why? Because we don't go through the storm alone.
The God of the storm walks into the wind with us. He
holds our hands, picks us up when we fall, carries us
when He must. And He leads us gently toward brighter
skies and peaceful days.

In *Miracles in Tough Times* you will see the God of

the storm in action as He calms life's turbulent waters, rescues the drowning, and carries the fainthearted to safety.

In Chapter One we see "Beyond the Clouds" when Roy and LaVerne are capsized into a rushing river and are headed straight for the waterfalls. Don is terrified when the cruise ship he and his students are on begins to sink. And Pamela is surprised when they find an envelope full of money on their porch just in time for a Christmas that had looked dismal.

Greg receives an unexpected miracle while "Searching for Hope" in Chapter Two. Susan finds silent faith while watching her deaf child at play. And Nancy discovers the truth about fairy tales in the midst of life's attacks on her.

"Keeping the Faith" is the theme of Chapter Three, and not an easy task. Tom is unstoppable even after he develops a severe case of asthma. And Angel inspires her sister with hope while losing her own hair to chemo.

In Chapter Four, "Waiting for Sunrise," Carol and Nate are trapped in the middle of a raging flood. A stranger stops the cappuccino machine at Starbuck's with a glorious song. And Marcia is enlightened through eyes that could not see.

Donna sees the hand of God at work when her car is stolen in Chapter Five, "Dreaming of Tomorrow." And

Rebecca discovers that the music of life still plays, even when times are tough.

If you're going through tough times of your own right now, we pray that you will find the faith and hope to go on as you read these true stories of other people who have struggled and survived. Just try to remember that the God of the storm loves you, and He'll be there to see you through to brighter skies and more peaceful days.

MARY HOLLINGSWORTH

MIRACLES
in Tough Times

CHAPTER 1

Beyond the Clouds

*The L*ORD *defends those who suffer; he defends them in times of trouble. (Psalm 9:9)*

Have you ever flown on an airplane on a cloudy day? The plane climbs up and through the dark clouds, and then suddenly you emerge above the clouds into bright blue skies. Beneath the clouds, the world seems dreary and gray, because the sun is obscured. But beyond the clouds, the sun is shining, and the world seems bright and happy. Tough times are clouds of our lives, bringing dreary feelings and sadness. If we hang in there, though, and keep climbing out of our pits, beyond the clouds we will find the sun shining on us again. Look beyond the clouds!

It All Depends on How You Look at It

BARBARA J. FISHER

I was blind! It was only for six weeks, but it seemed like an eternity at the time. Strange though it may seem, while I was blind I "saw" the people in my life more clearly than ever. My "disability" taught me to look with my heart rather than with my eyes.

At the time I was in a Columbus, Ohio, hospital, feeling scared, alone, and homesick for my husband and five children. I'm sure the darkness exaggerated these feelings even more. I spent hours, even days, wondering if I would ever see my children's faces again.

When the nurse told me I was getting a roommate, I was really displeased. Ironically, I didn't want anyone to "see" me this way. But, like it or not, my roommate, Joni, soon moved in to the bed next to mine.

In spite of my best efforts to dwell in self-pity, I almost immediately started liking Joni. She had a positive attitude, was always cheerful, and never complained about her own illness. She often sensed my fear and depression and had a knack for raising my spirits. She joked that I was lucky not to be able to see myself in the mirror. (My hair was a mess from lying in bed for a week, and I had gained several pounds from the cortisone IVs.) No matter how sad or angry I felt, Joni could always make me smile.

When Joe, my husband, would come to visit, he sometimes brought all five children with him. It was quite a challenge for him to dress five kids, all under six years old, and they often came to the hospital in mismatched outfits. After they were gone, Joni would tell me the specifics of what each one had worn. Then she would read each "I love you" and "Please get well soon, Mommy" from the cards they had brought.

When friends sent fresh flowers, Joni described them to me. She would open my mail and tell me how lucky I was to have so many friends. At mealtime, she would help me find my mouth with the food. Again she convinced me that, just for the moment, perhaps I was lucky to be blinded so I couldn't see the hospital food!

One evening Joe came to visit alone. Joni must have sensed our need for privacy; she was so quiet I wasn't sure she was in the room. During his visit, Joe and I talked about the possibility that I might never see again. He assured me that nothing could change his love for me and that, no matter what, we would always have each other and would continue to raise our family together.

For hours he held me in his arms, let me cry, and tried to make my dark world a tiny bit brighter.

After he left, I heard Joni stirring in her bed. When I asked her if she was awake, she said, "Do you know how lucky you are to have so many people loving you? Your husband and kids are beautiful. You are truly blessed."

I knew that during our weeks together in the hospital Joni hadn't had a husband or child visiting her. Her mother and minister came occasionally, but they only stayed a short time. I suddenly felt very selfish. I had been so wrapped up in myself I hadn't even allowed her to confide in me. From her doctor's visits, I knew Joni was very sick, but I didn't really know with what. I'd heard her doctor call her illness by a long Latin name, but I had never asked what it meant. I hadn't even taken the time to inquire. I realized how self-centered I had become, and I hated myself for it. I turned over and started to cry. I asked God to forgive me. I promised that, first thing the next morning, I would ask Joni about her illness, and I'd let her know how grateful I was for all she had done for me. And I'd be sure to tell her that I loved her.

I never got the chance to say those things to Joni. When I awoke the next morning, the curtain was pulled between our beds, and I could hear people whispering nearby. I strained to hear what they were saying. A minister was repeating, "May she rest in eternal peace." Before I could tell her I loved her, Joni had died.

I learned later that Joni had come to the hospital for that very reason. She knew when she was admitted that she would not return home. Yet she had never complained and had spent the final days of her life giving hope to me.

Joni must have sensed her life was ending that night when she told me how blessed I was. After I cried myself to sleep, she had written me a note. The day nurse read it to me that morning, and when my vision came back, I read it again and again myself:

My friend,

Thank you for making my last days so special! I found great happiness in our friendship. I know that you care for me, too, "sight unseen." Sometimes to get our full attention, God must knock us down—or at least make us blind. With my final breath, I pray that you will soon be seeing again, but not especially in the way you think. If you can only learn to see with your heart, then your life will be complete.

Remember me with love,
Joni

That night I awoke from a deep sleep. As I lay in bed, I realized that I could vaguely see the brightness of the tiny nightlight along the baseboard. My vision was coming back! Only a little bit, but I could see! But, even more important, for the first time in my life I could also see with my heart. I know that Joni had been placed in my life for that very reason. Even though I never knew what she looked like, I am sure she was one of the most beautiful people in the world. And though I never told her I loved her, I believe she knew.

I have lost my vision several times since then, but thanks to Joni I will never allow myself to "lose sight" of the important things in life. Things like warmth, love, and sometimes even sorrow, if shared with someone special, can be beautiful. It just depends on how you look at it.

An Angel's Visit

NANCY B. GIBBS

It was a beautiful day in June, while I was driving down a quiet highway, when a thought came to my mind. Everything in my life was pretty good. I had nothing really big to worry about. It almost frightened me when that particular idea came to mind. For it seems that just the time we feel like everything is going well the greatest storms come our way.

A few months later, as I expected, everything changed. I lived some sixty-five miles from my parents. Fortunately, I had kept my part-time job in the city from where we had moved and from where I grew up. So I had ample opportunities to visit with my parents.

My mother began telling me odd things that my father was doing and saying. Initially, I thought she was imagining things. Daddy couldn't possibly believe the things he was saying. She told me how Daddy was becoming paranoid and simply not acting like himself. He was still a young man, so I tried to ignore the warning signs.

But soon I had to face the facts. The doctors began

using scary words, such as "Parkinson's disease," "dementia" and "Alzheimer's." As frightening as those words were, however, they didn't compare to the words "terminal" and "final stages."

From that time on, my relatively calm life was transformed into a massive whirlwind. The doctors put Daddy on medication, but the drugs only caused him to become more paranoid. The medication also caused him to hallucinate, which in turn caused him to become violent. I have to admit that those were some of the toughest days of my life.

Knowing I had only a short time left to let my father know how much I loved him, the trips I made to my hometown increased from twice a week to sometimes six times a week. The only day during the week I allowed myself to rest was on Sunday. And that was only because my husband, Roy and I were serving at a small country church. We had to be there. Roy was the pastor. I taught Sunday school.

I went from having nothing to worry about to being totally stressed out. I didn't slow down. I couldn't slow down. I had been told my father only had a few months to live!

The family advocate at the hospital talked candidly to me one day. It was his opinion that Daddy would live much longer than everyone thought. "Your father has the heart of a twenty-year-old, Mrs. Gibbs," he explained. "But he has the mind of an eighty-year-old. Your family has a long road to travel."

He was right. Months turned into years. Those years were not quality years, however. Daddy became bedridden and quickly came to the point that he rarely responded to us. He didn't even know us. He resided in a nursing home for several years. Daddy experienced many painful days and nights in that place. And the whirlwind of emotions took a toll on our entire family.

After a couple years, Roy decided that I needed a break. "Our anniversary is approaching, Nancy. Let's go out of town for a couple of days." I hesitated, but accepted. I worried about being far from Daddy and was concerned that Mom would need me. But I knew Roy was right. I had to get away.

We packed our bags and off we went to a wonderful park three hours from home. For the first time ever, we stayed in a bridal suite. The room was gorgeous and the weather was perfect.

The first morning there, we walked around the park, enjoyed the scenery, the gift shop, and the exhibits. I thought of Daddy and constantly wondered how he was doing. But I tried to stay focused on enjoying our anniversary, for Roy's sake.

We returned to our hotel room to get ready to go out for lunch. Roy left the room to get ice. I fell down on my knees beside the bed and prayed. "God, please send an angel to take care of Daddy," I whispered.

I heard the key in the door and knew that Roy had returned. I stood up and brushed away the winkles on my outfit.

"Let's go eat!" Roy enthusiastically shouted.

We had lunch and went shopping. I laughed for what seemed the first time in a long time. I felt a sense of peace.

We returned to the hotel later that day. I decided to call my mother to check on Daddy and to see what kind of day they had. My mom gave me an update. Nothing much had changed. But just before we hung up the telephone my mom stopped me.

"Oh yeah, Nancy, I need to tell you something that happened at the nursing home today. I went out to get Daddy something for lunch. When I walked back in the front door, a nurse met me. She told me a stranger was in Daddy's room and had been there for a while." I sat at the other end of the telephone speechless.

"They told me," Mom further explained, "that they were watching her closely since they had never seen her there before. I walked into the room and a stranger was praying with Daddy. When she concluded her prayer, she turned and looked at me."

Then Mom relayed the entire conversation to me.

"Hi," the young woman said, "I know you don't know me, but God sent me here. I live across town. As I was pulling out of my driveway, He guided me here." When she got out of the car in the nursing home parking lot, she said she asked God to show her which room to visit. "As I walked down the hall, He told me this was the room. So I stopped. I hope you don't mind."

My mom assured her that it was fine for her to visit and to pray with Daddy anytime. She hugged my mother. Before she left, she shared a message from God with my mom. "God said to tell you that everything is going to be fine."

When my mom hesitated, I asked her an important question. "Did this happen about twelve thirty?"

"It was about one when I got back to the nursing home," she replied. "Why?"

"That was the time I asked an angel to take care of Daddy," I replied.

"Do you think she was an angel, Nancy?" my mom asked.

"Do you have a better explanation for her visit?" I followed.

There was silence at both ends of the telephone for a few seconds. I was certain God had heard and answered my prayer. My mom was convinced she had encountered an angel earlier that afternoon. We both experienced a myriad of emotions. But in addition, we both believed the message God sent that day. "Everything was going to be fine."

Daddy never walked again. He didn't experience an instant and complete recovery. A couple of years later, however, Daddy left a place of pain and entered a place where he would never hurt again. And everything was finally fine with him.

Mom and I both knew then and have oftentimes talked about how an angel visited Daddy's room that day. As far as we know, this kind lady never returned to the nursing home to visit with Daddy.

But somehow I believe a miracle occurred on the day Daddy left this world behind and entered the gates of heaven. Who knows? This angel just might have been sent by God once again, to escort my father home.

Toward the Brink

ROY DENIAL

I was on vacation with my wife, LaVerne, camping in the Great Smokies of North Carolina. We were going to spend the day river rafting. As we unloaded our gear, LaVerne grinned at me, her blue eyes carefree. *I wish I could be more like that*, I thought.

I had started my own business some years earlier, after the firm I'd worked for relocated to another state. We lived in Detroit then; it had always been my home, and I wanted to stay put. I had plenty of contacts, and I used them to help get my public relations and marketing firm off the ground. But my position weighed heavily on me. It was no longer just a job; now I had an entire company to be responsible for.

LaVerne pitched in by keeping the books, and after only a year I was able to hire a full-time artist and a writer, as well as some part-time help. We were doing all right for ourselves. So well, in fact, that one day LaVerne said, "Let's not grow anymore," after she'd tallied the latest figures. "We're fine."

Yet something drove me to take on more and more clients. After all, bigger is better, and I had enough experience that I was sure I could handle the load. But the work started to take its toll. I traveled so much that often I woke in the morning and wondered, *What city am I in today?* And if I wasn't out of town, I put in so many hours at the office I was exhausted by the time I finally dragged myself home. LaVerne begged me to slow down. So did my son, Eric. He wrote me a letter from college, which read in part, "Please don't work so hard, Dad. You don't have to prove anything. . . . I love you and want you around." I knew how much my family cared, but the business wouldn't run itself. Besides, I didn't think it was killing me.

Now, as we stood on the bank of the river with nothing but free time, the last thing I wanted to think about was work. Wearing bathing suits, LaVerne and I dragged the raft through ferns and wood sorrel to the water's edge, setting it down in a cove of crystal-clear water that rippled gently over mossy rocks. I hauled the fishing rods from the car and LaVerne grabbed the picnic basket and camera, and we loaded up the raft. For safety's sake I always double-checked an unfamiliar river before we launched. "Be back soon," I said, heading to the car. I slipped behind the wheel and glanced at LaVerne. She was sunning herself on a rock, her hair shining as if it had been polished, looking every bit as pretty as the day I first fell for her, back when we were teenagers.

As I drove, I thought about our many vacations, and

how much that time together meant. Years earlier, before I started the business, LaVerne had given me a rubber four-seat raft, which was more affordable than the boat I'd been yapping about. "It floats, Roy," she'd joked. That it did. With our children, Eric and Marsha, we'd rafted all over the country. Now the kids were grown and off in college, and it was just LaVerne and me.

That old raft will do fine on this river, I thought. Not much white water, just the kind of easy ride we're hoping for. Every once in a while I pulled over to check the depth and strength of the current. About two miles down there were some flat rocks on the near shore, and the opposite bank jutted out like a fish's belly, forming a bend in the river. *Nice spot,* I thought. *I bet it'll look real pretty on our way past. We'll go farther downriver, then we can picnic and fish.*

When I got back to our launch site LaVerne was leaning against a tree, trailing a bare foot in the water. "Everything okay?"

"This river has just enough punch to be fun," I told her.

We climbed into the raft and paddled out of the cove. When we hit open water, right off I felt the strong current.

"Some punch," LaVerne said, sounding a touch nervous.

"Don't worry," I assured her. "We'll be fine."

But the landscape whizzed by a bit too fast. We worked the paddles hard, trying to steer clear of the rocks. The water foamed around us. Something's wrong here. This isn't what I saw from the road.

Too late I realized my mistake: That fish-belly jut of land ahead was actually an island. What I hadn't seen earlier, from the far side of the river, was the treacherous stretch of water hidden around the bend. We were being propelled straight into rough water. There was a near-deafening rumble, above which I could barely make out LaVerne screaming, "Waterfall!"

"Lord, help!" I cried, realizing we'd never make shore. I shouted to LaVerne, "Crouch low in the middle of the raft and hold your paddle!" then reached to pull her down next to me.

We were at the mercy of the current, just seconds from the falls. Fear roared in me, louder than the river. We hurtled toward the brink, clinging desperately to each other. Then we went over the edge. We smacked down with a jolt that practically shook my teeth out. Gear flew everywhere. I caught a glimpse of the camera about a foot from the raft, just before it was swallowed by gray froth, along with our fishing rods and picnic lunch. Miraculously, LaVerne and I hadn't been thrown out. We sat up, sputtering. Seeing calm water and a rocky shore just fifteen feet away, I started paddling frantically.

It was no use. Surge after surge of water pummeled

us. My paddle was ripped from my hands. Just then we were hurled downriver, away from the waterfall, but right into a whirlpool. The raft spun wildly, faster and faster, trapped in the inexorable grip of the suction. Any second we'd be pulled under.

My life had boiled down to this: one moment of terror on a remote river, my wife and I facing what looked to be certain death. All I could think about was LaVerne and our children, and how much I wanted to go on living for them. *Lord,* I prayed, *please don't let this be the end.* All at once I felt quiet and peaceful. In my mind I let go of everything. Whatever happened, the river wouldn't have the last word. God would.

LaVerne and I looked at each other. "I love you, Roy," she shouted above the din.

"I love you too," I shouted back, and took her hand.

Suddenly, inexplicably, the raft shifted. To this day I don't know how to explain it, but the raft shot out of the whirlpool and into the quiet water that had tantalized us when we'd slammed down at the base of the falls. Soaked and shivering, we sat dazed. Finally I climbed into waist-deep water and towed the raft, with LaVerne in it, to shore. I helped her out and we held each other for a long time.

The rest of our week wasn't quite as adventurous, but it was one of the most memorable vacations we've ever taken, because after we got home, I reconsidered how I'd been running my business—and my life. Rather than be pulled under by too much work, I decided to resign some of my accounts. Things ran pretty smoothly after that. God's message had been clear: Let go and leave it in His hands, just as I had that day on the river.

Drive-by Blessing

SUSY FLORY

C uba is a hot and sweaty place, but the people always look unwrinkled, unhurried, undusty; all of the "uns" that I couldn't seem to master on this mission trip. I don't know how they do it. Many Cubans own one shirt, and that single shirt is without fail spotless, pressed, and worn with pride. We Americans, on the other hand, were rumpled, cranky, and sticky.

At the tail end of a nine-day mission trip to bring food, medicine, and Bibles to needy Cubans, we were making one final stop, one last drive-by blessing. On this particular day, God led us to a small house church in the town of Candelaria. No one expected us. When we knocked on the door of the small, dusty house church, we interrupted a meeting of five Cuban missionaries, all in their twenties. We found out later that they were in the midst of fasting and praying for help.

They greeted the nine of us strangers with kisses on the cheek and murmurs of *"Gloria de Dios."* We entered, sat on rickety wooden benches, talked. They didn't act surprised. It was as if we were honored guests, fully expected.

One by one, the Cuban missionaries shared their stories. One had been a priest of Santeria. The peaceful glow on his face belied the scar on his hand, a relic of his blood initiation into the voodoo-like cult.

Another had been a street fighter, his bulging muscles clear evidence. "If it weren't for Jesus, I'd be insane, in prison, or dead," he told us.

Then there was Sandi. He had short brown hair, a close-trimmed moustache, and gentle chocolate colored eyes. His white pants and gray polo shirt were clean and looked like they had just been ironed. What I didn't see was that the seat of his pants was ripped wide open.

Sandi was a pastor's son, but rebellious. When his father began a house church in their home, he ran out the back door whenever it was time for a service and carried on wildly in town. He felt torn, however. One day, he broke down and began praying in the park; not long after he found the little Candelaria house church, where he surrendered to Jesus. He was discipled by the pastor, and two years later God sent him to a new town to start a church. His goal is to reach all one thousand people of his town for Jesus.

As Sandi spoke, I heard a creaking noise from the back of the church. The heavy church door bumped across the concrete as Doug, one of the men from our team, went outside.

Doug loved people. While the rest of us were like

Marthas, frenetic with meetings, bagging medical sup-
plies, or prepping for puppet shows, Doug could often be
found face to face with Cubans—playing catch with
neighborhood kids, greeting passersby out the window
of our van, or gleefully trying out his mangled Spanish
on pastors and church workers. As a result, Doug saw
things we didn't see. He saw hurting people who needed
a kind word. He saw kids who needed a friend. He saw
the rip in Sandi's pants.

In a few minutes, Doug headed back into the church
with a nice pair of pants, Levi's Dockers, fished from his
suitcase. While another Cuban missionary spoke, Doug
walked with Sandi to the back of the church, spoke a few
words in his trademark Spanglish, and handed him the
pair of pants with a quick hug. I didn't think much of it.
We'd handed out all kinds of stuff.

Soon, it was time for us to go. The stories of the five
praying and fasting missionaries touched our hearts, and
we dug in our fanny packs to give them some much-
needed funds. As we said our good-byes, Sandi stepped
forward. "Wait. I have something to tell you," he said, in
a voice with a bit of a tremble in it.

"Yesterday, I rode the bus for five hours to come to
Candelaria to pray with my friends," Sandi said, looking
around at the other four. "When I climbed up the steps
of the bus, the back of my pants ripped open.

"They were my only pants."

Again I marveled at how neat and pressed Sandi looked.

"I prayed," Sandi continued. " 'God, please send me a new pair of pants.' Then I got on the bus and came here."

He turned to Doug, eyes aflame. "I just want you to know that God answers prayer." Sandi's faith hit me like a hurricane. It was like a physical presence in the room, alive, a fire, not to be ignored.

"It's an upside down world with the Lord," a friend once said. I began to see the truth of it. The Cubans were rich and we were poor. They live on faith; we live on MasterCard.

Doug came over, weeping, and put an arm around Sandi's shoulders. The rest of us were silent, amazed, broken.

Sandi continued, with a simple statement that cut us to the heart. We heard it, but I still don't know yet if we understand it or believe it. He held up the new pair of pants: "God provides all that you need."

A Teacher's Nightmare

DON HUME

E verybody at the meeting spot at 3:45," I called out. We were on the cruise ship *Sea Diamond* on a spring break trip in the Mediterranean. I'm an English teacher at Marina High School in Huntington Beach, California, one of three teachers in the group of six chaperones. I had twelve students with me: nine girls and three boys.

Normally the foreign language teacher is the leader on these trips. She didn't come this year, so I was in charge. It was great to see the kids experience things they read about in books. On this trip we'd already toured the ruins in Ephesus, Turkey; visited the cave where St. John of Patmos wrote the Revelation; and just that morning went to Crete where we toured King Minos's Palace of Knossos near the legendary Labyrinth. The group reboarded the ship together at 11:30.

After lunch I instructed everyone to meet for our second departure that day, the island of Santorini, reputed to be the fabled location of the lost city of Atlantis. At 3:45 p.m. I stood at our meeting spot on Deck 6. I began a head count. Four girls weren't there yet. *Probably applying last-minute makeup or trying on a different pair of jeans.*

A grinding noise suddenly emanated from deep within the bowels of the ship. Then a shudder rippled through her and she tilted considerably to the right. "What was that?" one of the students cried out in alarm. "I think we just dropped anchor," I responded. I adjusted my footing then added, "She'll right herself." But she didn't.

We were in a sea-filled crater formed by a volcanic eruption thirty-five hundred years ago. Reefs were clearly marked with orange buoys and flashing lights. *We couldn't possibly have hit something!* Then a young girl sprinted toward us. "Get upstairs," she said. "Something's wrong." She patted her legs with her hands. It made a squishing sound. Her pants were soaked all the way up to her waist.

"Crew members are running up the stairs wearing life vests," Shawne, one of our female teachers, said when she locked eyes with mine. *We must have hit a rock!* Passengers dashed past our group and a swarm of people pounded up the stairs from the lower decks. I frantically scanned the area around our meeting spot for the four missing girls. *Where were they?* I had to get these kids to safety. "We'll take the stairs to Deck 8 where the lifeboats are. Stay together," I instructed.

We moved toward the steps, our angle slightly cock-eyed because of the tilt of the ship. A flood of wide-eyed passengers rushed madly by. We had all attended the muster drill when we boarded. Everyone knew to gather there in case of an emergency. But ours was at the front of the ship, and we were at the back. We crammed onto Deck 8 and pressed in with hundreds of others wedged side by side. The mob of passengers all had the same idea—find a way to escape.

"Should we go down to our cabins and get our life jackets?" a few of the kids asked.

"No!" I said emphatically. "Don't go back inside. Stay right here."

The ship listed about 30 degrees. Glasses placed on tabletops crashed to the floor, anything left out on a counter tumbled off. It was difficult to stand; one leg felt shorter than the other. We didn't hear an emergency warning or an announcement from the captain. I examined the sea of faces before me. About 30 feet away I spotted one of our adult chaperones. I waved wildly and got his attention. "Who's with you?" I hollered. He shouted the names of two of our girls. We were missing only Nicole and Jessica now.

Anxious passengers tore open the life jacket lockers on deck, the steel lids banged against the wall with a hollow echoing sound. They were empty. A murmur of fear rippled through the crowd. Then an announcement rang out: the watertight doors were closing up to Deck 3 in the bow of the ship. The first and second decks were flooded. Blasts rang out on the ship's horn. Three short, three long, three short. The S.O.S. distress signal.

An army of people jostled each other, pushing and shoving, as they groped their way forward to the lifeboats. Then word traveled like a wave: "Women and children. Women and children first." It passed from person to person, crew member to crew member. Along with all the other men on deck, I saw our boys take a step back. There were six lifeboats, three on each side. They loaded the closest women and children aboard and lowered the boats into the sea. Our group stood well behind the railing. The boats were full.

"The rest of the women and children follow me," a crew member shouted.

"Where are you taking them?" I yelled back.

"Deck 3. We'll evacuate from there."

Shawne gathered our five girls and the other female adults. "I'll take them below," she said. My mind screamed out for them to stay. I was in charge of this group, and I wanted us to stay together. At least then I knew where everyone was. *Except for Nicole and Jessica.* I stood with our three young men and watched the girls enter the ship; the boys' eyes filled with concern, and my stomach tightened with fear.

A few minutes later, the dad I had seen earlier elbowed his way through to us. He had his two girls with him and behind them was another. Jessica! A crew member guided the girls to the lower deck for evacuation. *God, the parents trust me to bring their children home safely. Nicole is still missing. She's got to be with somebody who will keep her safe.*

We worked our way to the railing and looked over the side. The Aegean Sea roiled, powerboats frantically roared up to the stern and waited impatiently, bobbing in the frothing ocean. "Mr. Hume, look! There they are," one of the boys cried out. One by one we watched our girls climb down a wet and slippery rope ladder. Waiting crew members plucked them off the rope and set them into a boat. Our first five girls and three female adults were off the ship. Then later, the other three girls. "They're safe," one of the boys said.

The ship lost power and now listed 40–45 degrees to starboard. We tried to keep our balance as the ship tilted more and more toward the depths of the sea. She was going under. And I hadn't found Nicole.

As a teacher, I have to be one step ahead, I have to know everything that's going on at all times. But here I was on a sinking ship, and there was nothing I could do. *God, this is in Your hands.*

I looked at these young men with me. It had been three harrowing hours, and through it all they had been brave and strong. The mass of passengers had funneled to a small flock. "Follow me," a crew member called out.

There was no way out but inside and down. I had to have faith that God would protect us. We entered the dark, cavernous ship. Except for the agitated murmurings of the passengers navigating their way down the stairs, the ship was eerily quiet. "Grab the back of the guy's shirt in front of you," I instructed. We groped our way along the walls, shuffling from Deck 8 to Deck 3, leaning substantially as the ship continued to tilt. The crew had mated a huge door, once used to load cars onto the ship, with a ferry boat. Planks were lined up to walk on. We joined the line and walked onto one of the last boats pulled up to the stern.

Suddenly my cell phone beeped. It was a text message from Shawne. NICOLE IS HERE. EVERYBODY IS ON SHORE BUT YOU GUYS. Nicole was safe! *Even when I didn't know where she was, God, You did.* I quickly sent a text back. ALL OFF. EVERYONE IS SAFE. I didn't need a cell phone to send my next message: *Thank You, God.*

Some of the kids were bummed for a little while over everything they lost: iPods, makeup, expensive jeans. Later, I heard the kids talking as the enormity of the situation sunk in. "That was all just stuff," I heard someone say. "We have each other."

I lost a lot of things too: my computer and all my photographs. But like the kids said, it was just stuff. I was bringing home each and every one of the students entrusted to my care. I knew that I was only a temporary keeper; that God watches out for all of us every day. He's the One who is always in charge.

Reach Out and Touch Someone

MARCIA K. LEASER

It turned colder during the night, and when I awakened it was snowing lightly.

This was my first winter in the country and I had no idea how quickly the narrow rural roads could be filled with wind-driven snow.

I bundled up my two daughters—Dawn, four, and Tammy, two—threw on my tennis shoes over bare feet, and headed for town. I arrived at Mom and Dad's around nine, and before I knew it, it was going on eleven. It had been snowing heavily for the last hour, and the wind had picked up also, but I didn't think too much of it as I pulled into the grocery store parking lot. Forty-five minutes later, with the back seat loaded with groceries, we headed for home.

The wind had been blowing briskly in town, but as I drove farther into the country it whipped the snow wildly from the ditches onto the road in front of me. The temperature had warmed up just enough so that the light fluffy snow was now freezing rain pelting against the windshield. I could hardly see our little road as I approached it, but I heaved a heavy sigh of relief when I saw the familiar green road marker rocking in the wind. Turning gratefully onto it I thought how glad I was to be only two miles from home.

Even with home so close, I was becoming more and more frightened as my small Comet plowed its way through the white world before me. I could hardly see beyond the front of the car as the howling wind relentlessly swirled the snow around me. Suddenly the road disappeared into a giant snowbank, and I felt the car jolt to a stop. I tried backing up, but my tires only dug deeper into the built-up snow beneath them.

"Now what are we going to do?" Dawn questioned anxiously.

I was really worried but couldn't let the girls know. "Someone will come along," I answered in a cheerful voice, trying to sound hopeful. But deep down inside I knew better. No one would be traveling along that snow-covered road for a long time.

I was new to the country, but I was also new to other things as well. I had just become a Christian and was trying very hard to learn God's mysterious ways. I closed my eyes in prayer, asking Him to send someone to help us. The wind howled relentlessly, as if mocking my feeble prayer. The icy rain was hitting the windshield and freezing as quickly as it hit. The wipers were losing the battle at keeping up, and it was becoming impossible to see outside at all. I felt like a prisoner in a wicked world of white. Everything looked like a wrinkled sheet through the ice-crusted windows. Suddenly I noticed the gas gauge was on empty. Even as I sat looking, the engine coughed and died.

Within minutes the cruel wind had chilled the tiny car.

"I'm cold," Tammy said softly. You could see her breath before her as she spoke.

"What are we going to do, Mommy?" Dawn asked with wide, questioning eyes. Her voice quivered with cold.

I tried to think of a comforting answer. My mind was whirling as I remembered the giant snowplow that flew down our road, and my heart beat wildly. There was no way they would see my little white car half buried in that snow bank.

"We'd better walk home," I said in an encouraging tone. Home couldn't be too far ahead, I reasoned to myself.

I opened the door and was startled as I saw the door pushing the snow away as it opened. The snow had to be a foot deep or more. I grimaced at the cold as my bare ankles hit the bitter cold of the endless blanket lying before me. The wind-driven sleet stung my face as I stood with Dawn beside me. "Hang onto my coat," I yelled over the howling wind. "And don't let go," I added in a warning tone.

Her eyes searched mine. "Are we going to be all right?" she asked nervously.

"Of course, honey," I assured her with a smile. Then added, "The Lord will take care of us." The words sounded foreign. I wasn't used to speaking in terms of faith. I felt better having said them, though, and was surprised to realize I actually believed it.

Grabbing Tammy in my arms, I noticed a single tear on her tiny cheek. Kissing it away, I covered her with a blanket and carried her close. I could feel her little body tremble with cold, but she remained calm in my arms.

"Let's go!" I shouted, as I took one last look at the week's supply of groceries in the back seat.

The snow was so deep that little Dawn could hardly walk, and the vicious wind hurled the stinging rain against her reddened cheeks. Thank God she had her long woolen scarf to wrap around her face and the hood of her heavy coat to keep the sleet from hitting her neck.

After only a short distance my feet were completely numb. Turning around I was shocked at the fact the car was hidden from view by the whirling snow. I wasn't even sure we were traveling in the right direction.

"Oh, Lord, please help us!" I cried into the emptiness before me.

Suddenly, I heard voices—men's voices. I could see nothing but white and wondered if I was hallucinating. But wait! Looming in the distance, barely visible through the wind and rain, was a huge gray truck. Telephone repairmen were working on the lines.

"Help us! Please, help us!" I screamed out through the whistling wind. Within seconds, Tammy and Dawn were being whisked up into huge, strong arms, and I felt the warmth of the truck's cab as they pulled me into it.

They took us home, which was only a quarter mile down the road, but I doubt we would have made it on foot. As we entered the house, I glanced at the clock. It was two. We had been out in that awful weather for over an hour!

Not only did the telephone men take us home, but also they returned to my car and brought all my groceries to us as well. I never even asked their names, but God knows, and I'm sure they will be rewarded.

Later, curled up on the couch, wrapped up in my nice warm afghan, the girls and I discussed our ordeal. I don't think they realized the seriousness of the situation, but I did, and I was thankful to be alive.

I learned a lot that day: First, wear heavy boots, hats, and mittens when traveling in the winter. Secondly, never underestimate the weather, and start for home before the roads become impassable. But the greatest lesson I learned was this: There is a caring, loving, heavenly Father who hears our prayers over howling vicious winds. And even though He doesn't always calm the storm, He'll send help to bring us safely home.

Chicken Dumpling Soup, Turtles, and a Miracle

PAMELA KESSLER

T he snow made a hollow, crunching sound as I marched around to help my first-grader out of the car after school. His excitement for Christmas was as bright as the orange crop of hair on top of his knit cap-laden head.

"Mom, I can't believe we'll have a white Christmas!" He scooped up a mitten full of fresh snow and bit into it like a crisp apple.

"Matt, don't eat the snow," I said.

He licked a last bit of his snow snack and whipped it down on the ground. He had no idea of our financial crisis since my husband had lost his job a few months earlier. I didn't know how I would be able to get gifts for him, let alone the rest of my extended family.

We trudged up the ten steps to my mother's large frame house where we rented the basement apartment.

"It will be easy for Santa to land his sleigh in this snow."

"I suppose it will. What are you hoping Santa will bring you this year, son?"

"Turtle action figures and the van to put them in too!" he exclaimed in one breath.

As if I didn't know.

We stumbled through the front door burdened with coats, boots, a turtle backpack, and other winter paraphernalia. Matt sang part of the theme song from the turtle cartoon program and dumped his backpack in the front hall.

He skipped into the kitchen where my mother was heating some water for tea. "Hi, Gram, do you have any cookies?"

My mom gave him some cookies and milk, and away he went to watch the turtles on TV. It was his favorite show. He had some of the action figures, pajamas, slippers, sheets, and a comforter for his bed. His cousin was also into the turtle rage. They played together all the time, and he wanted the same things for Christmas.

"Mom, I don't know how I'm going to be able to afford Christmas this year," I said and slumped down into the chair at the kitchen table. "My bills are behind, and Tom makes half as much as he did at his last job. There's just no money for Christmas."

"Don't worry about it, honey; it will work out," she said in her motherly wisdom.

But I didn't share her positive outlook. Christmas was just a couple weeks away, and I didn't have any shopping done.

"Just make sure you have gifts for Matthew," she added. "Don't worry about the rest of the family."

"I know, but I don't have anything for him either, and I just don't have the money. Plus I feel bad because he's been so sick this winter. Every time he turns around he seems to have strep throat. We even had to cancel his birthday party, remember?" I leaned back in my chair and sipped my tea.

We sat and stared at the kitchen table as if it held some solution to the problem.

Mom tried to change the subject to our Christmas Eve plans with the family, what we would serve, who would bring what food, and then the subject of money made full circle right back to where we had left off.

"I don't know how I'll be able to get gifts for the kids when they come over on Christmas Eve." I felt numb.

"Don't worry about it; everyone understands," Mom consoled.

But it didn't help.

"Well, I guess I'll go downstairs and get supper started. Oh, I'm making Grandma's chicken-and-dumpling soup tomorrow. I'll make it up here and we can all eat together, if that's okay."

"That will be great, honey," Mom said.

That night after supper my husband, Matt, and I sat around our little Advent wreath and had devotions from a booklet Matt had gotten in Sunday school. He put the sticker in the booklet that was all about the town of Bethlehem and the special things that were in the stable where baby Jesus was born. We said our prayer and Matt blew out the Advent candles. I tucked him into bed and we read a Christmas book about the real Gift of Christmas—Jesus. Then I snuggled the covers around him and kissed him good night. He pulled his turtle comforter up over his turtle jammies, leaving only his orange hair and little nose exposed.

When I went to bed that night I thought about our financial situation and uttered a prayer that God would help me focus on the real meaning of Christmas and to trust Him that things would work out. I repeated the verse from Proverbs: "Trust in the LORD with all your heart and lean not on your own understanding; in all your ways acknowledge him, and he will make your paths straight" (Proverbs 3:5–6 NIV).

I didn't have the money, but Christmas was not about money. I left my concerns with God and prayed that things would work out as I focused on the real meaning of the season.

The next evening we were sitting in Mom's kitchen eating our chicken and dumpling soup. Matt was complaining about it because he didn't like soup.

"Can't I have a grilled cheese sandwich?" he begged.

While we were discussing grilled cheese the doorbell rang.

"I'll get it!" Matt jumped out of his chair in a last ditch effort to get out of eating his soup.

"Sit back down, Matt. It's dark outside and we don't know who it is, so we'll let Dad get it." I said. "Now eat some soup."

Matt plopped down in his chair and reluctantly picked up his spoon. He stared into his bowl of soup and sighed.

My husband went to answer the door and went out onto the porch. He came back inside walking in zombie fashion, reading a note.

"Who was it?" I asked.

"I don't know."

"Well what is that note? Who brought it?" I urged, thinking it might be about an overdue bill.

"There wasn't anyone at the door—just this note that says 'Merry Christmas to the Kesslers' with two hundred dollars inside." He leafed out two, crisp hundred-dollar bills.

"What?" I was speechless.

Matt bounced up and down in his chair. "Wow, two hundred dollars!"

Tom handed me the card with the money inside, and sure enough it was as he said.

"And you didn't see anyone leaving the porch or outside in a car or anything?"

"Nope, I looked around but didn't see anyone."

I passed the card around while we tried to think of who would do such a kind thing.

"Do you have any idea who might have left the money?" Mom asked.

"No, not a clue," I said.

Our conversation for the rest of the meal was trying to figure out who might have left the gift and of our amazement over the whole incident. But inside I was pondering why I was so surprised that God would answer my prayer.

We were so thankful for the anonymous kindness and generosity of someone who was moved by God to share with a family in need.

Christmas morning was exciting as we witnessed the enthusiasm of a little orange-haired boy as he opened his turtles and the van to put them in too. He received his special gift, but I received the greatest gift—a renewed trust in a God who loves His children and answers their prayers in wonderful, personal ways.

A Dilemma—
To Go Home or Not

DEMARIOUS BEAVER

Here I am, twenty-eight years old, a widow with two young sons. There was another, my middle son, Austin, who lived only two years. His grave is near my husband's in Indian Territory.

"Are we nearly there?" a small voice asks.

"Yes, we're nearly there," I call to my children. "Come on, boys, I know you're tired, but so am I."

My back aches from the heavy bag that I take turns carrying or dragging. The boys wag sacks crammed with as much as they can carry. I'm thankful for the kind old couple that helped us across the White River on the ferry. Papa had built the ferry years ago, and many people, wagons, and carriages have used it to cross the river for as long as I can remember. Down the path is our old place overlooking the river.

From a distance the cedar log house, surrounded by sheer limestone cliffs, looks the same as it did when I was a girl. It was built years before the Civil War and is only a few miles from Pea Ridge Battlefield. The home befriended many soldiers in its day, and General Price had been a guest there. I was a little girl, but I remember that he sat by our fireplace with his head down gazing into the fire. Our house was a stagecoach stop, and at times served as a hospital during the war.

I see the window of my upstairs room. Many nights my sisters and I whispered secrets in that room and giggled over silly unimportant things. We had a close family, but when Mama passed away, things were never the same. She died a few days after the birth of her tenth child, who also died. I was nineteen. A year later, Papa met and married a widow from Berryville. I couldn't accept another woman in Mama's place. Two months after Papa's marriage, I eloped with a doctor ten years older than I. We lived in Eureka Springs for about a year, then traveled deep into Indian Territory and settled in the Choctaw Nation. My husband was the first white doctor. There, we were among others who had run away from one thing or another— mostly men who had run from "the law."

I walk toward the house with halting steps. It will soon be dark. The old twisted plum tree reaches out to me as I pass by. I see myself as a young girl picking plums from that tree along with my brothers and sisters. From the buckets of ripe plums, Mama made delicious jelly. I remember its sweet, tart flavor.

My youngest son is whimpering, reaching for my hand, and I don't have the energy to pick him up. I can't control this feeling of uneasiness and dread creeping over me. The house seems too still and quiet—maybe nobody is home. But there are sheets hanging on the clothesline. They wouldn't go away and leave a washing hanging on the line.

Will Papa welcome me? I doubt it. He had not wanted me to marry, and when he sees me, what will he say? It has been two years since my husband passed away, and I'm still grieving. These two years have been the toughest times in my life, not knowing from one day to the next if I would have food for my children. Friends and neighbors in our Choctaw community helped. Finally, I had no choice but to make the trip from Indian Territory back to the place of my childhood, to Papa's house in northwestern Arkansas.

I need to get hold of myself. I'm determined not to cry, but the tears come anyway. Hesitantly, I knock on the familiar door and wait. It opens. There stands my formidable Papa, looking much like I remembered him, with his thick shock of hair and bushy eyebrows. Surprise shows in his eyes, and for a second I think he might smile.

"Papa," my voice quivers, "I need help. Surely you've heard that my husband passed away. It was two years ago—pneumonia."

"Yeah, that's too bad," he mumbled.

A voice from inside asks, "Who is it?" I see the shadowy figure of my stepmother inside.

"Wait a minute," Papa says to me as he closes the door. I stand on the doorstep and wait. The rise and fall of quarreling voices reach my ears. Again the door opens, and Papa's piercing eyes tell me what I had already suspected—that I am truly not welcome in his home.

"You can stay here one night," he says firmly, as he glances at the two young faces behind me. "Tomorrow you must leave."

"I'll leave in the morning," I say with a sinking heart and without looking at him.

Suppertime is awkward with little conversation. There's a lump in my throat that won't go away. Neither Papa nor my stepmother sits with us at the long table, although there's plenty of room. They busy themselves waiting on us as if we're company. I feel uncomfortable and pick at my food. In spite of the tense atmosphere, my boys eat like they're starved. They take second helpings of pinto beans and buttered cornbread, and drink their fill of sweet milk. Suddenly, the kitchen door flies open and my youngest brother dashes in from his chores. The room lights up and my boys take notice.

"Is it really you, Joseph?" I jump up and grab him.

"They call me 'Joe' now. I'm sixteen you know," he laughs, as he hugs me.

"Sure enough?" I ask in disbelief.

"Sure enough! We've all grown up, De. You've been gone eight years."

Joseph glanced from me to Papa and our stepmother.

"What's going on?" he asked me with raised eyebrows, "Civil War?" I nod.

"What can I do to help?"

"Nothing," I whisper, "You can't afford to be on the losing side. I want to hear about our brothers and sisters." We talk until my boys are nodding and dozing in their chairs.

"I'll help you get the boys upstairs," he offered, "and make a place for you to sleep. Your room is a storeroom now. We'll have to move a few things."

"Thanks, Joe. You're a shining light in a dark place." He smiles.

The night is long and I sleep very little. I expected too much from Papa. He hasn't forgiven me for leaving home when he had four children left to care for. And I haven't forgiven him for marrying so soon after Mama's death. He needed me then, and I need him now. What else could I do but come home? It would be different if Mama were still alive. She would help me. And where will I go tomorrow with my children who have lost their father?

In the morning, I thank Papa for breakfast and reluctantly say good-bye to my brother. I retrace my steps down the path that I had walked the evening before, the same path I had skipped down many times as a young girl. My children follow obediently. I'm sorry for the feelings between Papa and me. One day we will make peace with each other; I know it. But today is not that day.

When I reach the ferry landing and am out of sight of the house, I plop my bag down on the ground and sit on a stump.

"Dear Lord, what will I do?" My eyes sting and tears roll down my cheeks. With elbows on my knees and head in my hands, I cry my heart out, moaning and praying. My children lean on me and hug me, but still I weep bitterly. And they cry too.

Suddenly, I hear a rattling sound of a wagon and horses approaching. With my head down, I hope that whoever is in the wagon will ignore me and not stop. That's not likely, since anyone who comes here will be waiting for the ferry, just as I am. The wagon stops and a man calls out, "Need a ride?" I wipe my eyes and nose discreetly on my skirt tail and manage a weak, "Yes, sir."

He hops down from the driver's seat, lifts my bag into the back of the wagon, and helps us in. The children settle among the bags, and I sit beside the driver. In a few minutes the ferry arrives and we board. We cross the White River in silence.

As soon as the wagon wheels roll onto dry land, doubts fill my mind. "What am I thinking? I don't even know where we're going!"

"Stop the wagon!" I suddenly blurt out. Immediately, I climb down and sit on a log by the road. Again I start to cry, knowing I have nowhere to go. The driver quietly takes in the scene—a situation that he clearly had not expected. He looks at my two solemn little boys in the back of his wagon; he looks at me, their distraught mother sitting on the log. He climbs down and sits beside me. Tearfully, I pour out my heart to him. He listens to my story with his head bowed.

"It's my turn," he says as he lifts his finger to silence me, and says, "My head is spinning from what I have just heard. Only this morning I was feeling sorry for myself, being single and sometimes lonely. I looked over the little group at church and saw families sitting together—men, their wives and children. It made me feel isolated and a little envious. Now, I feel like a blessing has just fallen on me."

He starts to reach for her hand but looking down at his rough carpenter's hands, stained from hard work, he decides not. She is taking in his every word. He clears his throat and continues, "When I saw you and your children, there was obviously something missing from that picture—a protective husband." He hesitates, "I'm only a carpenter, but . . ."

His words ring like a bell in my mind, "only a carpenter." He tells me he's a carpenter and my heart lightens. *Jesus was a carpenter,* I think. What is he saying?

"But if you will have me," he stammers, "I'd like to be your husband, and a father to your children."

We married and moved south near Fort Smith. Over

the years, four other children were born to us, two boys and two girls. It wasn't a coincidence that a compassionate young single man happened to find himself a "ready-made family" that morning. How else could it be, but for God's will, that we two people should meet on the side of the road on that day? God is always in charge, even when we don't have a clue as to what is happening.

CHAPTER 2

Searching for Hope

For in the day of trouble he [God] will keep me safe in his dwelling. (Psalm 27:5 NIV)

One of the toughest times in life is when you don't know where you are. You're lost. Alone. And you have no idea how to find your way back home. You wander around in circles, looking for anything familiar, some landmark or person to give you a hint about which way to go. You're searching. Searching. Searching for a signpost or something to give you direction. Searching for hope. And what a relief it is when that familiar person or place finally comes into sight! Your heart is lighter. Your step is quicker. A smile springs into your eyes. And hope is suddenly restored as you say, "Thank You, Lord, for leading me home."

Green Grape Pie

JEAN BELL MOSLEY

Old Man Pack lived in an abandoned chicken coop. He was allowed to stay there as long as he mowed the owner's lawn. This was during the Great Depression, when any roof over your head was a good one. Pack removed the pole roosts, salvaged the lumber, and made himself a bunk bed. He painstakingly collected the cleanest straw he could find and stuffed it between two ragged blankets to make a mattress. "I mixed in some pennyroyal and mint stalks with the straw," Pack proudly told me. "It gives the bunk the sweetest of aromas."

That was Old Man Pack for you, reveling in even the smallest luxury, even though he was worse off than any of us. So many things those days were a chore, from finding enough soap chips to do the laundry to finding new ways to prepare the same bare-bones meals for my family. I often got frustrated. But Pack never did.

One spring day Pack arrived at my kitchen door with a "Good day, madam." He had made our home a regular stop on his route, going from neighbor to neighbor asking if they were willing to trade any table scraps, or a sliver of soap perhaps, in return for odd chores. If you said you had nothing to spare, Pack would simply bow gracefully and say, "I do understand. Truly I do." He never made you feel sorry for him. I looked forward to his visits.

"Good day, Pack," I said, brightening just a bit. It had been a hard week, and today especially I couldn't wait to hear of his latest triumph.

"Madam," Pack continued, "would you make a green grape pie for you and me?" He had to be joking.

"Sure," I answered. "That's a great idea. My family hasn't eaten meat in two weeks, but I'll make us a green grape pie. Then maybe you and I can sit in the shade of my apple tree and eat it, while I wonder where our next square meal will come from."

"Your grapes are about at the right stage. It would be a shame to let them go to waste." I could hardly believe my ears, but he wasn't joking.

"Pack, do you know how much sugar it takes to make a green grape pie?"

"Yes, madam, I believe I do," he said. "About two cups' worth."

"Well, where on earth are we going to find that much sugar?"

Pack's face darkened. "I just thought we could do it," he began. "That pie would have tasted so good."

"Pack, you are a dreamer." And who could afford dreams?

"It's okay, madam," Pack conceded softly. "I do understand. Truly I do."

But I had disappointed him. Pack always seemed to come along when I was at a low point. Hearing him go on about how grateful he was to the Lord for providing his thirdhand kitchen range or pennyroyal-scented mattress had given me hope when I didn't think I had any left in me. Now here I was wrecking that same spirit I depended on. Pack had already gone a few steps down the walk, head held high.

"Wait!" I called, stopping him in his tracks. He turned around and came back up the walk. "Okay, Pack, we'll do it. I don't know how, but we'll do it." Pack's eyes lit up. "Shall we say two weeks?"

Pack nodded in agreement and said finally, "One cup of sugar apiece."

I closed the front door. I had no idea where Pack would possibly get his sugar. But I immediately got very creative with finding mine. I started in my own house. My husband put sugar in his coffee every morning, but wouldn't stir it. When he finished drinking, I'd spoon out the leftover wet sugar and let it dry.

By the end of fourteen days, I figured I'd have about one eighth of a cup of sugar. If I did without sugar on my breakfast cereal for fourteen days, I'd have another fourth of a cup. That would leave five-eighths to go.

I made a list of everyone who lived nearby, marking

down those with large families who might need soap powder more than sugar. I asked them all if they'd trade a half cup of sugar for one and a half cups of soap powder. No one would. A week and a half into my project I didn't see any way I'd make it. *Lord,* I prayed, *show me a way.*

On day twelve I was standing at the counter in the grocery store, waiting for the clerk to finish filling an order. The customer had requested sugar, and when the clerk lifted the paper sack of sugar to put it into her basket, the sack sprang a leak. All the "white gold" began to spill out! I quickly cupped my hands under it.

The clerk got a new sack and remeasured the sugar, while I stood there, my two hands full. "May I have this?" I asked with as much dignity as I could muster. The clerk simply shrugged—he couldn't very well sell the sugar now—and gave me a paper sack to put it in. I held my head as high as Pack and walked out triumphant.

On the fourteenth day, Pack knocked at my kitchen door, paper bag in hand. Though I'd worried about meeting my own quota, I never doubted he'd meet his. Pack's sugar was lumpy and tan-colored. There were even some splinters in it that I had to pick out. I didn't ask questions. My sugar didn't look so great, either.

Later that day, in the shade of my apple tree—except for the two pieces I set aside for my family—Pack and I ate the whole green grape pie. We savored every crumb in silence. It was hard to believe we'd only added two cups of sugar, because that was the sweetest pie I'd ever tasted. I was now a coconspirator in one of Pack's many small victories. *This is what hope feels like firsthand,* I thought.

Pack looked at me, a smile forming on his face. "I believe you understand. I believe you truly do understand," he said. And I did. I understood that God puts certain people in our paths. He put Pack in mine to show me that when you get a little creative and hold tight to your faith, you can do the impossible. And hope finds a breeding ground.

From the depths of the Great Depression right up until today, I meet life's challenges with the indomitable, unshakable belief of Old Man Pack. No matter the circumstances, there's always a chance for sweet success. I do understand. Truly I do. Because I baked a pie that proved it.

An Unexpected Miracle

GREG ASIMAKOUPOULOS

Four months after September 11, 2001, I faced my own Ground Zero. As I arrived at work that day, I had no idea what awaited me. I poured a cup of coffee, turned on my computer, and began organizing my projects for the day. My mug was still half full when, without fanfare, the boss promptly called me into his office. Whereas some might have taken that as an unmistakable cue, I didn't. It was not uncommon to be invited to an unplanned meeting to offer constructive criticism on a marketing concept. But when I was asked to sit down and the door was closed behind me, I began to get a funny feeling in my gut. He told me that eleven positions were being immediately eliminated. Mine was one of those. There would be four more weeks of pay, and a letter of recommendation if I desired. I was thanked for my contribution over the past half decade and wished good luck.

"And, oh, by the way," he said, "you can spend the rest of the day packing up your office or take the rest of the day off and return on the weekend to collect your personal belongings."

My heart began to beat double time. My stomach knotted to half its size. I was speechless. It wasn't that I didn't have things to say, I was too angry to risk opening my mouth for fear of what might come out. After five years with a family-run ministry, I felt entitled to a bit more warning than, "This is your last day with us."

A year earlier, I had been called aside and told that several positions might have to be eliminated to balance the budget. I had only asked for the courtesy of as much warning as possible. A day's notice was hardly that. As I cooperated with the compulsory handshake, I managed a smile.

I then shuffled back to my desk and dialed my wife. While the phone was ringing, I was clueless how to break this unexpected news to her. When the answering machine picked up, I asked Wendy to call me back. Breathing a sigh of relief that I did not have to admit to being a failure for a few more minutes, I rehearsed in my head how best to tell her.

As I waited for my wife to respond to my message, I proceeded to call on my heavenly Father for help. It wasn't much of a faith-filled prayer. It was more of an honest venting of hostility and fear.

When Wendy finally called back, I didn't try to soften the reality of what had happened. I just told it to her straight. Her reaction surprised me. After expressing an element of surprise, she calmly said, "Well, sweetie, we're on an adventure. These were five good years, but the Lord must have something even better in mind for the next season of our lives. I can hardly wait. To tell you the truth, I'm excited."

She may have been excited, but I certainly wasn't. Still there was something about her confidence that got me through the rest of the day. Two days later as I swallowed my pride and stood in line at the unemployment office, I tried to digest Wendy's assurance that God would bring about something good from this. But in all honesty, my faith got stuck in my throat.

Over the next few weeks I met with some friends and avoided others. Ashamed, I just wanted to hide. Besides, when people attempted to put a spiritual spin on what I was going through, I just wanted them to shut up.

I tried to process my pain in the pages of my journal. When you lose your job, you feel like Job. It seems you've lost it all. The world looks gray and colorless and tastes like bitter gall. You seek the Lord, but He won't speak. You lose your will to pray. And when your "good" friends try to help, you wish they'd go away. Quite insecure, you doubt your worth. You try in vain to hope. You feel alone. You feel afraid (without the means to cope). It's so unfair to be laid off. You gave your heart and soul. While others loafed, you sacrificed to reach your boss's goal. Your sleep declines. Your bills add up. Resentment stays the same. You don't know what or who to call. You don't know where to aim. No business card. No payroll check. You have no place to go. Without a job or business car, you feel like just a big "zero."

Our eleven-year-old daughter, Lauren, heard my wife stressing over the mounting expenses that accompanied my unexpected loss of employment. How were we going to make another month's payment of our oldest daughter's tuition at a private Christian college? How were we going to stay current with the thousand-dollar-a-month insurance premium my employer had been making on our behalf? When was I going to sell another article to a magazine to cover this week's groceries?

My wife had reason to be concerned. Without a job and no prospects in sight, my only hoped-for source of income was what I could make from freelance writing assignments editor friends would throw my way. As we entered the season of Lent, I didn't feel the need to identify something I would give up. The most important thing had already been taken from me. The weeks leading up to Holy Week were long and discouraging.

On Maundy Thursday evening I went out the front door to greet the evening sky and get some fresh air. As I turned to go inside, I noticed a little woven basket on the porch. Taking it inside I called Wendy and the girls to come and see.

The first thing that caught my eye was a little wooden cross tucked in the Easter grass. Then I saw five different colored plastic eggs. They were the kind we used to fill with jelly beans and hide for our three girls when they were younger. As I opened one up I saw a ten-dollar bill. My heart started to beat faster. Sure enough. Each egg contained a ten spot. Without hesitation, we circled as a family as my wife led us in a prayer of gratitude.

Thank You, Lord Jesus, for this unexpected reminder that You know our needs and that You are capable of taking care of us, Wendy prayed. *Forgive us when we start to worry and forget Your promises to provide.*

There was no note or any indication of whom it was from. Talk about a miracle. In the stale and somewhat scary atmosphere of joblessness, it was a breath of fresh air my spirit needed. The fifty dollars were funneled toward the expenses of that week's groceries, since we had a family staying with us. The little wooden cross was hung on the wall in our hallway.

"Let's keep it up all the time as a reminder," Wendy said. "Every time we see it we can remember how the Lord surprised us with what we needed."

On Good Friday as we prepared to go to a communion service, I couldn't help but reflect on the unlikely means God chose to provide for my spiritual bankruptcy. And there on the wall was a little cross reminding me that God is capable of rectifying my other losses.

As weeks without full-time income gave way to months,

Wendy and I took to the mat against twin wrestlers by the name of fear and insecurity. Our tag-team attempt to maintain a positive outlook proved sporadic. Fortunately on days when I felt like I was locked in a half-Nelson, she was up. On days she felt pinned to the mat, I had a praise song on my lips.

It was amazing. For several weeks I had a seeming endless string of unsolicited articles that were purchased by magazine editors. With excitement we waited for the mail to come each day to see if there was an acceptance letter or a check. Little by little we were paying our bills. But then there was a dry stretch. Wendy, already returning to the job force for the first time since we had children, began to stress out. Where would the money come from?

Hearing her mother's plaintive cry, Lauren, with confidence in her voice, said, "Don't forget the cross, Mom!"

My wife wrapped her arms around our youngest daughter and thanked her for her timely reminder. There was no need to worry. The cross was all the proof we needed that a permanent job and provision in the meantime was just around the corner. A tangible object hanging on the wall became a symbol of hope.

As weeks turned into months, that symbol of hope on the wall gave way to evidence that God had not lost our address. I was offered opportunities to write for a number of magazines and publishing companies. My work as a freelance writer began to prosper. My wife acti-

vated her lapsed credential as an educator and proceeded to gain a reputation as a substitute teacher. She
was requested so often, her assignments were almost
full-time. We didn't miss a mortgage payment or a college tuition bill.

Thinking with the Heart

SUSAN LUDWIG

I am a substitute teacher, and one day recently I was assigned to a grade 5/6 class at a city elementary school. After checking in at the front office, I walked into the classroom. The students' chairs were stacked in a pile near the window. Lesson plans were on the teacher's desk. The chalkboard had a welcome message on it. It all smelled to me of a typical, mundane Wednesday in my substituting life. I couldn't have been more wrong.

The first student in the room that day arrived in a wheelchair, and I quickly assessed that she had no use of her arms or legs and that she was hearing impaired. Laura wore glasses and had a narrow, pretty face. A paraprofessional, whom I figured was assigned to work one-on-one with the girl, wheeled her to the back of the classroom and immediately began tending to her. I left them alone and read the day's lesson plans.

In time, I wandered over and introduced myself. The sign language interpreter, who had shown up a moment or two after Laura and her aide, filled the girl in on who

I was and why I was there. Laura looked at me and smiled, and her aide told me that Laura communicated only with her eyes—a blink for "yes," two slow blinks for "no"—and that her intelligence was not at all impaired.

Students eventually streamed into the classroom, and their loud, excited voices were typical of preadolescents at 8:25 A.M. By now, Laura, her aide, and the sign language interpreter were seated at what looked to be their regular spots in front of the classroom. Laura was stretched out in a large reclining chair, her wheelchair now folded in a corner. Most, perhaps all, of the students took a moment and greeted Laura and the two adults with a quick and friendly "Hello" or "Good morning" or "How are you today?" Many took a moment to make eye contact with Laura, who could not voluntarily move her head to meet their gaze.

The morning progressed in what I'd consider a typical manner, and after the students came back from music class, I gave them ten minutes to read silently at their desks before lunch. Two girls immediately went over to Laura's chair and positioned themselves on either side of her. One girl read aloud from a book as the other girl used sign language to convey the story to Laura. The young signer's hand signals were fluid and seemingly perfect. Parts of the signing resembled a dance of her hands, and I was surprised at the beauty I found in the simple motions.

Occasionally, the girl who was signing would ask a question of Laura: "Do you like this book?" "Is it too boring?" "Do you think that Melanie will find her way home after this chapter?" The girl waited patiently for Laura to respond, and after interpreting the communication, she'd tell the reader, "Laura doesn't like the way this story is turning out" or something of that nature. The reader and the signer would switch places at what seemed to be prescribed times, each equally comfortable in either role.

At lunchtime, three girls and a boy stayed in the classroom to eat with Laura. I learned that she is fed through a tube in her stomach, and on the colder days, stays inside during recess. The students joked, told stories, and discussed television shows and schoolwork. The entire time, one student was always seated by Laura's head to relate what was being said by those in the group. Every so often, that signing student would report to the others, "Laura hasn't seen that show" or "Laura thought that was pretty funny." Occasionally, someone would move a tendril of hair away from Laura's eyes or adjust her glasses so they weren't crooked.

As I watched the students and their interactions with Laura that day, I was touched by this unique situation, and I wondered if the students knew how wonderful they were. For all the talk we hear about troubled children, these students really showed me an inspiring side of human nature.

And how fortunate, I thought, that in addition to learning how to turn fractions into decimals and about ancient Greece, these students are learning more. They're learning that the disabled are regular people. They're learning that they can think with their hearts as well as their brains. Indeed, their unconditional acceptance and affection for this particular student, and all of their fellow students, may turn out to be one of the greatest lessons these children will ever learn.

Silent Faith

SUSAN FARR FAHNCKE

He came into this world chubby, bald, beautiful, and with the bluest eyes I'd ever seen. After a very difficult delivery, he was born perfectly healthy, and we all breathed a sigh of relief. We named him Noah and it seemed to fit.

The day after Noah was born, the nurse came into my hospital room and told me it was time to take him for the newly implemented newborn hearing screening. I thought this was a good idea and watched as she wheeled him away, thinking I could use a few moments to myself. I didn't know that this simple test would forever alter our lives.

She handed Noah over to me a short time later and informed me that he failed the hearing test, but that it was nothing to worry about. Often newborns have fluid, which block their ear canals. It happens all the time. Another test was scheduled, of which I was assured Noah would pass with flying colors.

A week later we returned to the hospital for the second test. Again, there was no response. The audiologist reassured us that it was probably nothing—leftover fluid, or just complications of testing such little babies. Another test was scheduled for two weeks later. I thought the waiting would kill me. Two weeks is an eternity when you are waiting to find out if your child cannot hear.

Returning home, I took Noah to his room for his nap. I looked around the room and suddenly everything took on a new meaning to me. The musical Noah's ark mobile above his crib—could he hear it? The books that made sound to go along with the story—would they mean anything to him? The lullabies I sang to comfort him when he cried—did he even know? I felt the tears splashing down my face and was powerless to stop them. I looked at my tiny, pink-cheeked boy, fast asleep, and wondered what his future would hold. I softly stroked his cheek and said a silent prayer that it was all just a mistake.

The next appointment came and I had to go alone. My husband was out of town on business and there was no way for him to be with me. We talked about rescheduling the appointment, but decided against it. We had waited too long already. With shaking hands, I took him in and watched as the audiologist once again hooked the machine up to his ears. He was silent as he tested Noah, not giving me any indication of what he saw. Finally, he unhooked Noah, and without looking at me said, "It appears that your son is deaf. You will need more tests to make sure, and I am scheduling you to see a specialist." He never once looked at me, but just wrote in his chart as he delivered the news.

I stared at him in shock. This wasn't real. It just wasn't happening. I felt numb as I tucked the appointment card into Noah's diaper bag and carried him out of the hospital and to our car. Like a robot, I got in and started the car. *Deaf. Deaf. Deaf* pounded in my head and I couldn't make sense of it. My car phone rang and it was my husband. Hearing his voice finally made it real. I pulled over to the side of the road and just sobbed into the phone.

"Noah is deaf" was all I could get out. I heard my husband's voice on the other end of the line crack as he tried to comfort me and then broke down in tears himself. "I'm coming home now. I'll get on the next flight." We cried together for a few moments and then hung up. He was on the next flight home, and we spent the following few days in a numb, disbelieving state of shock. We never imagined that we would have a child born with what other people call a disability, and it brought us into a world that we hadn't planned on and that was completely unfamiliar to us. We felt simply helpless.

Having a child born unable to hear was not what I had dreamed. My visions of the future were forever changed with the diagnosis. "Noah is deaf" rang over and over in my head until the words finally sank in. My heart broke for the things he would miss—things like the sound of a bird singing on a warm summer morning; the way music can fill your soul; the sound of his own children's laughter. My voice. And the things that would keep him safe—a fire alarm, a horn honking, the doorbell. I couldn't stop focusing on what he would miss.

Then I began to pray. My prayers at first full of self-pity, fear, and anger began to take on a new sense of peace. Prayer can do that to you. Hope filled my soul like a sweet melody.

The thought came to me that there had to be programs, schools, something for deaf kids. We immediately decided as a family to learn sign language. I had taken two semesters of American Sign Language in college and had never known why I had such an impulse to learn the language. Now I knew why.

I began to search the Internet for programs for children who are deaf. My search began to bring one delightful surprise after another. I met a woman named Shirley, who became my very dear friend. Shirley is deaf, and also very active in the deaf community. She was a Godsend. She introduced me to people, told me about programs and schools and other families with deaf kids. E-mail began pouring in from all over the country. People who were deaf wrote words of encouragement, told me of this program or that program. I began to see that Noah had a bright, promising future ahead of him. I felt like spring inside.

I met and became friends with many people who became my lifelines. Any questions I had, they answered. Any fears, they allayed, openly and honestly.

Knowing so many deaf adults who were very successful in their chosen careers showed me that the possibilities for Noah were endless. I began to grasp that the only thing Noah couldn't do was hear. Everything else was possible.

God sent so many people into our lives to help us find the way for Noah. Once I began to pray and ask for help, He sent it in tremendous blessings.

Noah now has a best friend his age who also is deaf. Her name is Renate. They will grow up together and be lifelong friends. When they are together, they have their own little language—half sign, half Noah/Renate special lingo. The tiny hands flying, expressions animated, it is a sight to behold. There is nothing more beautiful, no language more complete.

In order to become more proficient at signing, our family instituted new routines to help us. Tuesdays became "no voices" day. We simply turn off our voices and only communicate in sign. Each and every night, without fail, we sit together as a family. We do not talk; we only sign, and we discuss our day with each other. Each family member takes a turn telling the best things in their day and the worst things. It has brought our family incredibly close to one another. The children tell us things they never used to, and they also learn a little more about their parents that they wouldn't have known before we instituted nightly "family time." We did this primarily to become better at talking with Noah, but the extra closeness and blessings are more than we ever expected to gain from it.

We end every night with family prayer, and now that Noah is old enough, he frequently offers the prayer. To watch his chubby arms and hands give thanks to God for his blessings; to watch him say "thank you" for his mom, his dad, his brothers and sisters, his fishy crackers, for trains, his cat; to ask the Lord to give us good dreams—all are a work of art to me. Often my eyes fill with tears and my heart overflows with gratitude for this amazing child. None of us would change Noah in any way if we could. His deafness makes him who he is. He is happy and beautiful, and he brings blessings to everyone he meets.

A new world of wonderful and amazing people, and a beautiful flowing language began to open for us. Our family united in a way that we never would have, had Noah been born "normal." Our faith in God was rewarded tenfold. Noah's jubilant spirit brought us into a world of great beauty, of an appreciation for living, for family, for our faith. They say that trials in life will make you stronger. Having Noah was the epitome of that and more. Our faith increased by the small miracles along the way. Our hearts were opened and filled in a way that could only have come from this great gift in the tiny package.

The Truth About Fairy Tales

NANCY JO ECKERSON

I grew up in the sixties—a very different time. Like most of my girlfriends, I read and absorbed fairy tales as if they were fact. For sure, Goldilocks and Little Red Riding Hood were never really in danger because we all knew the bad guys got it in the end, and innocent heroines and heroes always prevailed. There was no debating the issue.

It was just a matter of the protagonists learning their lessons, and then the good stuff would pour down from heaven. Once the moral was gleaned, everything would go from black and white to color again, and rainbows would bejewel every sky. Rich princes would appear and whisk the captive away. The evil, plotting knave, usually dressed in black, would be carried off to exile. There was never a doubt. No villain ever triumphed.

Snow White won the war against her wicked stepmother, and of course, once Dorothy came to realize there's no place like home, she was speedily returned to her dear Auntie Em. Every little girl and boy had a champion like Glinda, the good witch of the north, standing in the wings, ready to assist in any disaster.

I had a fairy tale picture of my noble white knight too. As a young girl I conjured up swooning fantasies of TV's Dr. Kildaire falling madly in love with me. I was so sure that I was destined for a great love that I started a Dr. Kildaire fan club and was honored to be appointed president right away.

A year or so later, I had a new dream in which I met Peter Noone of Herman's Hermits who, the very second he laid eyes on me, was smitten for life. Starting his fan club seemed the right thing to do. I knew that I was truly destined to lead the life of a rock star's girlfriend. Since I had always dreamed of being a famous singer, it was an obvious match to me. I was cut out for greatness.

Then I grew up. I witnessed injustices that might not ever be reconciled. I sustained abuse in ways I could never have imagined and became ostracized and bullied by the "in" crowd at school. Although I was angry, I always tried to do the right thing, feeling it would eventually ensure a happy life.

I went to college to guarantee that I would be financially successful for the rest of my life. I was tempted to quit and get married at the end of my sophomore year, but my parents convinced me to finish, knowing that all

I needed to be protected forever was a university diploma. Apparently, my parents did pay attention to the man behind the curtain—the wizard of Oz. During those years of college, I learned about families all over the globe with no homes, no food, enduring the kind of violence that would scar deeper than mere physical signs might show. Had anyone ever promised them fair treatment?

Life changed dramatically after yet another series of traumas obliterated my expectations of a charmed life. All within a two-year span, I was assaulted, raped, and beaten in Europe, devastated when my fiancé left me without a good-bye, and then given the news that my mother had been diagnosed with Alzheimer's at age forty-nine. With a pronounced limp in my personality, and devastating pain and resentment in my heart, I stumbled on through the next couple of decades. I made some very bad choices in those days, based on my weakened state. I thought I was a helpless victim to the graying of my world and the fading of my hopes. I stumbled over each and every rock in the road, becoming more and more incapacitated.

The realization that life is not always fair, even when you play by the rules had now planted itself like a huge boulder in my path. It loomed large and dark, blotting out the sun. This is not the promise of Snow White and her handsome prince. What ever happened to "happily ever after?"

Discussions at my local exercise club often evolve into tirades about the unfairness of life. The members unanimously agree that no one had ever promised life would be fair.

But I protest! I was trained from infancy that it would be fair in the end . . . wherever and whenever the end was, either here on earth or maybe even in heaven. I have grown up believing that somehow life is going to work out in favor of harmony and peace—on the side of justice and right action. If you have faith, you believe that everything works together for good.

As my instructor wisely touts to all the pragmatic naysayers, "Don't give up. It ain't ever after yet." I find myself being pulled toward that enlightening fact. I allow the spark to rocket me out of my anger and despair, renewing my hope. My memory is refreshed, as I realize that those few words mirror my own life-long philosophy.

I have given up and gone cynical more times than I care to recount, but the real truth is, I still believe in miracles. My world is overflowing with them every day. God somehow comes to my aid each and every time I get discouraged, sending signs of a pure and loving world. A backyard filled with red cardinals against stark-white snow shows me. Watching a newborn baby stretch in the maternity ward convinces me. And, no matter what current circumstances may be, I know I am never far from feeling that there is a reason to celebrate living found in every single day. The only way we really lose is by giving up. And I can honestly say, as long as I am living I'm holding out for the happily ever after!

I have gone from agoraphobic to adventuresome, from divorced to delighted-to-be-alive, and from a three-pack-a-day smoker to healthy and singing in the choir again. My belief in God and miracles, small and large, has brought me to a joy-filled existence.

The Hardest Prayer
I Ever Prayed

MARCIA K. LEASER

I*ntensive care* rang in my ears, as I bounded across the crowded parking lot to the hospital entrance. Rushing into the elevator my eyes frantically searched the directory for the correct floor. Completely numb, I pushed the proper button.

I knew Dad hadn't been feeling well, but not this. Not a heart attack! Tears fought to be set free, but I quickly suppressed them as the elevator slowed, then jolted to a stop. I had to be brave for Mom, who was waiting just beyond those doors. They opened to reveal a place that would become very familiar during the coming days. Mom was sitting in the tiny waiting room looking lost and alone. She busied herself by jotting notes to friends and loved ones, as if she could keep the awful truth at a bearable level by writing the news on paper.

Sensing my presence, she stopped her nervous pen.

"I'm glad you're here," she said with a strained smile.

I thanked God I lived close and could come so quickly. I managed a smile too, not wanting her to know how frightened I was.

We sat silently without tears, expressions telling all with eyes staring, seeing nothing. My mind was on Dad. He was a big man of sixty-four, who had worked his entire life. I knew how much he'd hate being confined like this.

The sign on the cold metal door leading into Intensive Care read: Visitors limited to immediate family only. Ten minutes allowed for each visit at two-hour intervals, from 10:00 a.m. to 8:00 p.m.

Before my arrival, the nurse had given Mom a list of rules telling us what to say and how to act, so as not to upset Dad in any way. We were to appear hopeful and not make any reference to the machine above his bed monitoring his heart. Everyone's heart is different, she explained, and since neither Mom nor I were heart specialists, we could in no way understand the device. Talking about it in Dad's presence might upset him. Most importantly, we were not to allow him to dwell on the subject of money—who would pay for this and so forth. That was a tall order, for Dad was a worrier, with money always being a sore subject. And doctor bills were number one on the list of things you never mentioned!

I'd been there only a few minutes when it was time to visit Dad. It was hauntingly quiet and the very air took on a businesslike quality. We tiptoed into his room, not really knowing what to expect. He looked so pale against the sterile sheets. When had his hair gotten so white? It petrified me to see him so helpless. My dad—my big strong father lying in that bed with his eyes closed looking almost as if he was . . . was . . . my breath caught in my throat. I felt weak all over and wanted to run from this unkind truth that confronted me. I wasn't sure I was able to keep from taking him in my arms and sobbing. "Oh, God, please give me strength." My heavenly Father answered my hasty prayer, and with a grateful sigh I took Dad's hand. He responded with a smile. With that smile some of the awful fear left me. He squeezed my fingers and it seemed so good to be with him. The ten minutes went by quickly with Mom not saying much, just standing beside him holding his hand. Somehow she managed to keep the threatening tears at bay. I was so proud of her . . . of us, for passing a most difficult test.

My mind was busy with the usual questions one thinks of at times like this. Why Dad? He is such a kind man . . . oh he would get all upset over taxes and politics, but I never recall hearing him ridicule anyone in all my thirty-three years. I was brought back to the little room and the moment at hand with Dad laughing and joking about all the tubes and wires. "I sure am wired for sound," he said and because he hadn't lost his sense of humor, we left with a greater assurance of a complete recovery.

We returned to the small waiting room to discuss how to tell Peg, my younger sister. Chris (my older brother) had been called and was on his way from a neighboring state. Mom had purposely not called Peg, because she wanted to be with her when she was told. Peg was six months pregnant and had had two previous miscarriages. We decided to go together to the bank where she worked. Fortunately, she was on her coffee break, and we were alone. Peg had grown close to God in the past year, and we knew He would strengthen her. Blue eyes searched my face as I told her, then filled with tears. When we left, though, she was smiling and anxious to visit Dad on her lunch hour.

I left Mom then and went home. If only I'd awaken from this nightmare and discover nothing had changed! The next day we set up a schedule so Dad would have company every visitation hour. I went in at noon and six, Peg at two and four, and of course, Mom was there almost all the time. As I sat in the quiet waiting room, I silently prayed for God to strengthen Dad. I wanted to cry, but thinking tears were a sign of not trusting God and giving up, I constantly fought them back.

Being a holiday weekend, we hadn't talked to the doctor and just assumed the attack was light and Dad's heart had already started to heal. I didn't even know there were different coronaries. Some that healed . . . some that didn't.

By the third day things had become fairly routine. The big building had become a second home to me and even the usual eerie, uneasy feelings most people experienced upon entering a hospital had disappeared. I barely noticed the medicine odor anymore.

Stepping off the elevator this time, however, I knew something was wrong. Mom's face looked more drawn and her eyes had lost that look of hope I had clung to for the last few days.

"Doctor Gordan called this morning," she began hesitantly, "and explained what we are up against. Your dad is a strong man or he wouldn't be here now. But there's a problem with getting his heart stabilized; a blood clot went through his heart and about a fifth of his heart has been destroyed."

Destroyed! The word cut like a knife! I'd been so positive he was doing well. Before either of us was ready, it was time to visit Dad. How could we possibly be cheerful and optimistic when all hope had seemingly been lost? We swallowed hard, plastered on smiles, and walked in quietly. His morale was great, and Mom and I avoided all talk of his progress. That was the longest ten minutes I'd ever experienced, and I sank wearily into the nearest chair when we returned to the waiting room.

Mom looked tired, so I told her to go home and try to rest while I told Peg the doctor's report. On the way, I prayed for the right words. As I pulled into her driveway she came out to meet me. Still no tears as I explained the call Mom had received that morning. As we stood talking, my legs started shaking and I felt drained of all energy. Peg helped me into her kitchen and we sat at her table and prayed. We both knew Dad was in God's hands, and no matter what happened, He would give us the strength to bear it.

Driving home from my sister's house with spring all around me, the truth was too real. Dad could die!

"Oh, God, don't let him die." The road disappeared in a flood of tears and for the first time since I'd heard about Dad, I cried.

The words Peg had said just minutes before came at me from all directions over and over again. "We must turn Dad over to God completely. Whatever happens is His will. He alone knows what's best."

I hated to admit it even to myself, but I hadn't turned Dad over to God. I knew I couldn't change His will, but I suppose I was afraid what His will might be.

At home, I fell to my knees and prayed, "Father, he's Yours. Give me the strength to accept whatever Your will might be."

With that prayer of release came a peace only God can give. I knew whether Dad was healed to live an earthly life or an eternal one, he was safe . . . safe in the arms of Jesus.

Grocery Cart Angel

SUSAN SUNDWALL

B oy was I feeling sorry for myself. A good friend and her husband had just told us of their encounter with a waitress who wanted to know what Good Friday was all about. We were all ears as we sat in our Thursday morning Bible study, and a few others also related similar experiences where God had used them to help or inform others. As I listened, something in the back of my mind began to nag at me. *Why did these chance opportunities to bear witness to God's love never happen to me? Perhaps I was such a poor example of what a believer should be that I wasn't worthy of such moments.*

That nagging thought occurred again a few days later on my way to church as I sat at the traffic light next to the grocery store where I almost always stopped each week after services. My focus diverted for a few seconds, and I did a quick note-to-self to run in for the Sunday paper, cold cuts, and milk on my way home that day.

Later, as I zipped through the store aisles, I thought about another phenomenon we talked about in the Bible study. The pastor spoke of looking at the world with our spiritual eyes so that we can see others as God wants us to see them. I paid for my paper, cold cuts, and milk and hurried for the grocery store exit. It was a beautiful summer morning, and I couldn't wait to get home and get on with the day.

As I passed through the automated glass doors, I noticed a woman standing on the sidewalk near a line of grocery carts. She tightly gripped one by the handle. Her face was a picture of agony. Her eyes were squeezed shut, her mouth hung open and tears oozed from her eyes. I slowed up for a moment, but here I have to say that I usually take little notice of other shoppers when I'm intent on getting home to a hungry family. I'm ashamed to say that my first thought was to rush past and head for my car. I almost turned away, but somehow I couldn't take my eyes off her face. This woman drew me to her for reasons I would only fully understand later.

"Are you okay?" I asked, approaching cautiously.

"No," she wailed, tears spilling down her cheeks. "I just talked on the phone to my father."

"Oh dear," was all I could think of to say. She wasn't a young woman, perhaps forty, and I wondered what about their conversation could have caused this outburst.

"He hates me!" She gagged the words out.

I looked around quickly to see if anyone else had noticed her distress, but the other shoppers were oblivious, scurrying by as though nothing were amiss. I moved a little closer.

"I'm sure he doesn't," I said, trying to be sympathetic.

Her breath escaped in big gasps, and it was then that I noticed the strong smell of alcohol. *Oh great,* I thought, *what was I getting into?* My mind went into overdrive. I could offer some kind word like "things will work out" and leave her there, or maybe I'd ask if I could call someone for her. She didn't seem like a street person. Her clothes were clean, her hair was combed, and she didn't have her hand out for money. She was a middle-aged woman in deep distress, and I was the one who had noticed. I felt rooted to the spot.

I stood with her for about twenty minutes as she told me the story of her stormy history with her father. Today she had only wanted to call and tell him happy birthday and got nothing but hostility from his end, or at least that was her side of it. I had no idea if what she was saying was true. I didn't give in to the temptation to mention her substance abuse as his possible reason for the hostility. In her next breath she also told me she'd just been released from the hospital. "They let me out too early," she said, "and I need my medication. I wish I was still there."

This gave me pause and more than a little anxiety. Now I wondered if I should call the rescue squad. During similar nerve-jangling situations in the past I had always looked for a way out, but this time, amazingly, I felt graced with a peculiar calm. Maybe it was because I was in a public place and could literally walk away without consequence. And this woman wasn't a friend or relative, so I had no real responsibility toward her. Or did I? The discussion at Bible study popped into my head. Was it possible that I was drawn to her because on some level I was actually using the spiritual eyes we had spoken of? I looked at her again and suddenly wanted to tell her how much God loved her. I made up my mind to do whatever it was that this poor woman needed.

"How did you get here?" I asked, ready to provide transportation if she asked for it.

"I have a car out there," she said, waving vaguely in the direction of the parking lot.

"Would it help if I took you home?" I asked.

"No, I don't live very far from here." She sniffed back a few more tears and looked around. "I think I'm feeling better now," she said. Then she smiled at me. "You're a very nice person," she said.

"Well, I hate to think of your being all alone," I said. "What can I do?"

"Thank you for just standing here and talking to me," she said, sighing. "I really love my father so much. I hope he has a happy birthday."

I leaned forward a little. "Do you know how much God loves you? He loves your father, too," I said.

"Sometimes I pray," she said. Her voice sounded less tear choked and she smoothed her hands over her dress.

It was as if she had come out of a fog and was now aware of her surroundings. "Is there a place in here where I can get a cup of coffee, do you know?" she asked, nodding at the grocery store doors.

I told her to look for the small lunch counter near the produce section at the back of the store. "Do you need some money?" I asked.

"No, I have money," she said, patting her pocket. "Maybe I can get a muffin or something too," she said, "I'm hungry."

It was then I realized that probably all she had needed was someone to listen to her. At that moment I did something I never, ever do with complete strangers, especially ones with alcohol on their breath. Just before she turned to walk away, I reached over and gave her a hug. "God really does love you," I said.

She hugged me back and wiped her hand over her eyes. She smiled again, straightened her shoulders, and walked through the automatic doors of the grocery store. I never saw her before or since, and in a small town like ours that's saying something.

It's only been a few years since I had that encounter with the grocery cart angel, and you may ask why I call her that. But, you see, I know that the methods by which God works don't always fit into our strict notion of what those methods should be. It's not hard for me to believe that I encountered a being in the guise of a disturbed woman with alcohol on her breath. The Bible says the first emotion one experiences when an angel shows up is fear. My grocery cart angel had indeed produced a fear in me, the fear (and annoyance) of stepping out of my own time constraints, for one. Remember, I had a hungry family waiting on me. I was also afraid that I wouldn't know what to say to her, and that fear was exaggerated when the scent of alcohol rose around me. But every fear took a backseat to the need the woman presented on that sunny sidewalk in front of the grocery store. When it was time for me to witness to His love, God gave me the words I needed to speak, and just like my friends with the Good Friday waitress, I was able to voice and, more importantly, to show the love He has for all of us.

It turns out in that particular encounter I was the needy one. Sure this woman needed to have a listening ear for her current woe. But as I stood with her I realized she was answering a need in me too. God had counted me worthy of sharing His grace with her. The angel at the grocery cart allowed me to step out of my own tidy world and into hers, befriending her for ten minutes on a busy Sunday morning. She helped me understand the necessary use of our spiritual eyes as the instrument God gives for seeing His way in the world.

CHAPTER 3

Keeping the Faith

Be alert. Continue strong in the faith. Have courage, and be strong. (1 Corinthians 16:13)

The Bible says, "Faith is . . . knowing that something is real even if we do not see it" (Hebrews 11:1). And when times are tough in our lives, sometimes it's easy to take our eyes off of God and lose *sight* of Him. Lose *sight* of the fact that He is real. In other words, we can lose our faith. Because we can't *see* Him in the darkness that surrounds us, we begin to wonder if He's really still there. Perhaps the key to keeping the faith in our darkest times is focusing our minds' eyes on the Light. Look for the Light of God at the end of our tunnels. And keep on walking toward the Light.

When Papa Asked God for More Mules

GUSTAVIA RAYMOND-SMITH

As the wife of a foreign service officer, I've traveled all around the world, living mostly in developing countries. When I looked at lush fields in Zaire or green rice paddies in Laos, I thought of the farm I grew up on in Natchitoches, Louisiana, with its neat rows of crops, the tall brown sugarcane shimmying in the breeze, the cotton blooming white like popcorn. I found that no matter how far I traveled, I took a bit of my childhood home with me, especially the bedrock faith of my father.

Jerusha was what my father always called me, using my middle name. "Jerusha," he'd say, "what did you learn at school today?" or "Jerusha, please get me a glass of water." Jerusha was the mother of a Judaean king in the Bible. Papa wanted us to have strong names so that we would stand firm against the adversities of life.

Papa couldn't read very well. He'd dropped out of school in third grade to toil beside his father, cutting trees and hauling logs to the sawmill. When he and my mother met he was working in a lumber mill. Then he bought the small forty-acre farm where they reared their children. With fourteen of us, Papa and Mama's work was never done. He labored in the fields from dawn till dusk, and she was on her feet all day in the kitchen or vegetable garden.

What Papa couldn't read about his faith, he more than made up for by living it. He was a deacon in his church and was often called upon as the song leader. He chanted each line in his mellifluous baritone and the congregation repeated it. At home he led us in a weekly prayer and singing time. We got down on bended knee in front of our chairs, sinking our elbows into the caned seats, our heads bowed, hands clasped. Then Papa spoke to God as though the Lord were right there in our front room with us: "Listen to Your children here on bended knee, calling on Your grace and mercy . . . "

Papa's first exhortation to us in the morning was a prayer. He and my brothers were up before dawn, feeding the animals in the barn. Then he came inside and called to us, "Rise, shine, give God the glory." We splashed water on our faces and feasted on breakfasts of eggs, bacon, grits, and Mama's hot biscuits.

As hard as things were in the 1930s, we knew we were fortunate. Ours was one of the few black-owned farms in the parish. Folks came to us to buy fresh vegetables or drink a glass of water cooled by ice chipped from a 100-pound block. Papa sold the main crops: corn, soybeans, and sugar. With the money he went to Mr. Nelkins's general store and bought shoes and fabric to be sewn into clothes for us. There were so many of us the neighbors used to tease my parents. When one lady spotted us gathered around the kitchen table, she exclaimed, "Look at all those chilluns. They can eat the heads off the angels and drink the Jordan dry!"

But we never went hungry. We had horses that got us back and forth from town and mules that helped with the heavy plowing and hauling. Some people were envious of Papa's success. One night our barn burned down in a suspicious fire. There were rumors about who did it and why, but the chances of a black farmer successfully pressing charges were slight. And, anyway, that wasn't Papa's way.

Early one morning I listened, half asleep, to the whistle of a passing train and the commotion my father and brothers were making as they tromped out to feed the animals. Papa's shout made me jump out of bed, wide awake: "The mules are gone!"

Our mules were part of the family. We had given them names—Mink, Squirrel, Pet, and Tilldi. They worked hard, and I think they looked forward to the trips into town as much as we did, pulling the wagons with the harvest to be traded for provisions.

I ran into the kitchen. Mama was stirring grits and

cutting biscuits. But there was no joy in the sizzling bacon or the steaming coffee. None of us could eat a thing till we heard about the mules. "Lord, have mercy," Mama kept muttering under her breath. And when Papa finally came inside, he didn't even utter his usual, "Rise, shine, give God the glory."

He sank onto his chair, tears rolling down his weathered cheeks. We children were shocked. None of us had ever seen Papa cry. Even when the barn burned down he hadn't shown any sign of discouragement. "The Lord don't give us any more than we can handle," he'd reminded us at the time. But now he looked like a beaten man.

"Rollie Raymond," Mama finally whispered, "what happened?"

"They're dead," he said. "The mules are dead. Run over by the train." Someone had opened the barnyard gate and let the mules out. They'd gone their usual route, following the train tracks to town. But without Papa or my brothers to guide them, they were killed by the locomotive.

Even though I wasn't much bigger than a bean plant, I knew how serious our loss was. It was planting time. We needed mules to plow the fields. If we didn't get the crop in soon, there wouldn't be any harvest and we wouldn't be able to pay the annual installment on the farm, not to mention barter for provisions at Mr. Nelkins's store.

That night we gathered on the front porch for an emergency prayer meeting. We sang as we had never sung before: "Amazing Grace," "Walk in Jerusalem Just Like John" and especially "He Knows Just How Much We Can Bear." We got down on our knees, our elbows on our chairs. "Dear God," Papa prayed, "You know how much we needed those mules. So, Lord, please give us a way to plant the crops and plow the fields . . . "

Papa borrowed a team of mules from another farmer for a couple of weeks until the man needed the animals back for his own plowing. After that Papa tried hitching up our horses, but they couldn't do the job. Every evening we gathered for singing and prayer. "God, it says in the Bible that faith can move mountains," Papa prayed. "I won't ask You for that much, but if You can see it in Your wisdom to give a poor farmer a few more mules . . . "

With all the courage he could muster he went to the bank. Perhaps he could borrow enough money for some new mules, using the farm as collateral. The owner of the bank turned down Papa's request with a flat no. Two days later Papa went to the mule farmer. Maybe they could work out a deal.

When we looked up the lane and saw the speck that was Papa coming toward us, we were filled with hope. Had God answered our prayers? As Papa grew closer, we could see his downcast head and slumped shoulders.

The news was bad. That evening we returned to our singing and praying with renewed vigor. "Jesus," Papa said, "in the parable of the persistent widow you showed us how God hears us when we are constant in our prayers. So tonight, heavenly Father, we come to You once more with the same request . . . "

"Amen!" we answered.

The next morning Papa went to the general store. He knew that Mr. Nelkins did not lend money—there was a policy against that. But maybe this one time Mr. Nelkins would make an exception. After all, Papa always paid his bills on time. Mr. Nelkins was a good, decent man. He would be sympathetic to Papa's request. Papa put on his best shirt and hat and headed into town.

I could hear Mama murmuring prayers as she ground meat for sausages. The rest of us prayed, too, while we were doing our chores—gathering eggs, drawing water from the cistern, hanging clothes on the line. I hummed, "He knows just how much we can bear . . . " *Well, Lord, I sure hope so,* I thought, *because we can't take much more than this.*

Finally I saw Papa's figure far down the lane. I squinted into the dust for some hint of what had transpired. Was he walking with his head held high and his hand swinging jauntily at his side? *Oh, Lord, let it be true!* When he was close enough so that we could see the expression on his face, he broke into a radiant smile. It was the most beautiful thing I'd ever seen.

"You got more mules!" Mama exclaimed.

"No," he said. "It's better than that. We've got a tractor!" True to his policy, Mr. Nelkins would not loan Papa money to buy more mules. But he agreed to lend him a tractor that we could pay for over time. You can't imagine how thrilled we were, especially my brothers. A tractor! It could do the work of a whole team of mules!

There was plenty of celebration and prayers of thanksgiving that night. As I bowed my head with my elbows on my chair, I listened to Papa and heard his faith at work. "Thank You, God. For a moment there I doubted You, but, while I was praying for mules, You had something even bigger and better in mind. A tractor! Thank You, God, in Your mercy!"

"Amen!" we all shouted.

The harvest was good that fall. Papa was able to make the annual installment on the farm, repay Mr. Nelkins, and had enough left over to buy us some good things to eat and fabric for new clothes. "Jerusha," Papa said, "don't forget what you learned here. God does not promise us a bed of roses, or even ice cream and cake, but He does say our bread and water shall be sure. He answers prayers." He does indeed, and I've never forgotten.

Trouble on the Rips

BILL IRWIN

I didn't have to ask my wife, Debra, if the river was high that April afternoon; I could hear it. The two dogs barked joyfully as we unloaded our canoe from the pickup. Pee Wee, our fifteen-year-old sheltie, jumped around my legs like a puppy, and even Bronnie, the big German shepherd, momentarily forgot his dignity as my Seeing Eye dog and tugged eagerly at the lead.

We had never had the canoe out this early, when the Sebec was swollen with snowmelt. But on that mild spring day last year, our friends Roland and Mary Richardson had suggested an eight-mile run from our town to Milo, the next town downstream.

They pulled their canoe from the back of our truck and followed us across the road to the put-in, where the foundation of an old mill jutted into the stream. Before Bronnie had led me halfway across the old mill floor my tennis shoes were splashing through icy water. I had never known the river so full!

"At least this should make the Rips smoother going," I said. The Rips are a 300-yard stretch of boulder-strewn rapids halfway between Sebec and Milo, the only tricky bit of navigation along our route. With the river in spate, I figured all but the biggest rocks would be safely underwater.

I held the canoe steady as Debra climbed into the forward seat. I'm the stronger paddler, so I always take the steering position in back. How can a blind man steer a canoe? people ask. And what brings me out on a swift-moving, rock-strewn river anyway? The first answer is easy; Debra directs me: "Left!" or "Hard right!" Why I do it is a harder question. Maybe it's because I know what it's like to have two good eyes and still end up on the rocks.

When I was a sighted person I was an alcoholic, a dropout as a husband and father, a guy who lived only for himself. The first clear-eyed thing I had ever done was as a blind man, when I asked God to take charge of my life. I had never spent much time in His vast outdoors, but after I quit drinking I couldn't get enough of it. I learned wilderness skills and became the first blind person to "thru-hike" the Appalachian Trail from Georgia to Maine. I made a point of telling fellow hikers about the God who guides me.

It was His world that beckoned as I took my place in the rear of the canoe, Bronnie between my knees, Pee Wee yipping excitedly up front. Then the two canoes were off along the deserted waterway. A few summer cabins, I knew, dotted the north bank, but there would be no one on this stretch of the river.

We chatted for the first few miles, before the thunder of the approaching Rips drowned out the Richardsons voices. The current picked up till our two canoes were careening along at breakneck speed. The roar of the rapids was so loud I could barely hear Debra, just a few feet away.

Abruptly, I felt us go into a spin, whirling round and round in a dizzying eddy. The motion must have startled Pee Wee—I heard him jumping about. Between my knees Bronnie jumped too. As his ninety pounds shifted, the canoe tipped sideways, then capsized. The next instant I was tumbling and thrashing in the middle of the freezing river.

I broke through the surface, shouted Debra's name, went under again. Something kept pushing me down. It was the canoe, forcing me underwater as the current propelled it downstream. Struggling free, I thrust my head up. "Debra!"

I snatched at the canoe, but the current tore it away. I hurtled through the water, slamming into boulders, rolling and spinning. As I bumped against a rock, I managed to grab hold. At that instant I heard over the roar of the water the sweetest sound in the world. Debra calling me.

"Baby!" I yelled. "I'm over here!"

She answered something, but the noise of the river

drowned it out. In the near-freezing water my hands were swiftly going numb. I let the current take my feet backward till they touched another rock downstream. Legs braced against the battering rapids, I shouted questions in the direction of Debra's voice. Though I missed much of what she said, I understood she had managed to haul herself onto a boulder, maybe five yards from the north bank.

"Have you seen Bronnie?"

"No!" she shouted back.

"Pee Wee?"

"He went under!"

Poor little fellow . . . Or maybe, I thought, as the icy torrent pummeled me, a swift death was easier than hypothermia's slow, inexorable shutting down. By the time I'd been in the water half an hour—I've got an uncannily accurate sense of time—my arms and legs were as numb as my hands. Milo was a good four miles away, but I was sure Roland and Mary had reached it by now. They must have realized we weren't following them. How long before they could get a rescue team organized? Maybe in time for Debra, but certainly too late for me.

Another half hour had passed when there was a cry from Debra. She saw Bronnie's body on the bank. No, she saw *him* on the bank! Bronnie, you made it!

By then I had lost all feeling below the neck. Debra was shouting something else. "I'm going to swim for it!"

"Don't!" I pleaded. Roland and Mary must have given the alarm by now. My internal clock ticked off another hour; the sun felt lower on my face. How much longer till rescuers reached us? Debra shouted again that she could make it to shore. "No! The Richardsons have help coming!"

"But they're gone!" she cried. "I've been trying to tell you! They tipped over right after we did!"

Mary? Roland? Gone? The first warmth I had felt since the accident was my own tears on my face. There was no hope for us either. It could be weeks before anyone opened one of the summer places. The next time Debra yelled she was going to swim, I didn't argue. "Okay, Baby," I called. "I love you!"

"I love you too! Here I go!"

Lord, keep Your arms around my wife!

For moments that seemed like hours there was nothing but the deafening tumult of the river. Then a joyful cry. "Bill, I made it! Bronnie's here! We're going for help!"

Four miles on a muddy logging road? "Good, Baby!" I called, though *Good-bye, Debra,* was what I meant. Running would at least keep her warm, keep her from having to see me swept from my rocky handhold. The fatal stupor of hypothermia was creeping through me, numbing my mind as well as my muscles.

Debra was gone maybe twenty minutes when I lost

my grip. The current whirled me downstream. A branch brushed my head and seconds later I stopped moving. There seemed to be tree limbs around me. Had I reached land? With barely any sensation in my lower legs, I pushed myself up, on my elbows, then onto my knees, until I was standing. I splashed a couple of feet forward onto flooded ground, then stopped. Directly in front of me, behind, all around, I could hear rampaging water. I must be on a tiny, half-drowned island.

A late-afternoon wind cut through my sodden clothes. My chance of survival, I knew, depended on creating body heat. Bracing my elbows on a limb, I began running in place in six inches of water. I had been at this hopeless marathon maybe an hour when above the water's roar I heard a shout from the bank. A man's voice.

"Hang on, help's coming!"

To my questions, he replied there were thirty feet of rapids between me and the shore. "Just keep running! Your wife's safe. The dogs too."

Dogs? Pee Wee made it? "What about our friends Mary and Roland?" I called to him.

"At our cabin. They're okay."

For another forty-five minutes, until the local game warden reached me in a canoe tethered to shore, I ran in place on my brushwood island, every step a prayer of thanksgiving. In the emergency room at the local hospital, Mary, Roland, Debra, and I pieced together the extraordinary series of events that had saved us. Fortunately, we were all okay physically.

Only two other people had been on those eight miles of river that day, a couple named Yanok who had come to open their cabin. They had been ready to leave when Albert Yanok, the man who called to me from the bank, for some reason went down to their dock. And there he had heard Mary calling for help.

She and Roland had ended up close to the Yanoks' place. Had the accident happened a minute later, had the Yanoks left a minute sooner, had Albert Yanok not been at the river's edge . . .

But, of course, someone else was on the river that day too. Someone who sees every picture whole. "We walk by faith, not by sight," the Bible tells us in 2 Corinthians. I knew it was true for the blind, but it's also true, I learned that April day, for the sighted. Each one of us is surrounded, every day, by an unimaginable network of people, circumstance, events. The totality is too big, too complex, for any but God to see it all. For the rest of us, the eyes of faith see best.

Unstoppable

TOM DOLAN

I took a breath and climbed onto the starting block. This was the race I'd trained my entire swimming career for. The finals of the 400-meter individual medley (IM) at the 1996 Olympics in Atlanta. I was going up against the seven best IM swimmers in the world. One was my rival and former University of Michigan great, Eric Namesnik. To win gold I would have to swim the race of my life. And then some.

I breathed again—as deeply as I could—and blocked out the thousands of people in the stands. The oxygen came slowly, as if I were sucking air through a straw. I have asthma, serious asthma. Also, an unusually narrow windpipe. Doctors say my condition limits me to about 10 percent of lung capacity. Meaning, I could breathe in only one-tenth the oxygen my competitors could. One-tenth. Imagine trying to keep up with a bunch of other race cars with a gas tank 10 times smaller. The hard part was getting here, I reminded myself. Now, for the final 400 meters.

I'd been working toward this moment since age five,

growing up in the Washington, D.C., area. I first jumped in the pool mainly to prove I could outswim my older sister. By seven, I was swimming year-round. My parents always taught us: You get out of life what you put into it. That's what I liked about swimming. If I worked hard, I'd win. Slack off, and I'd lose. It was that simple.

One cold winter morning when I was twelve, I was running around during recess. All of a sudden my chest felt tight and I couldn't take in any air. Kids gathered round me. "Tom, you all right?" I put my hands on my knees. Resting seemed to help. "Yeah, I'm fine," I wheezed. But I was done running for the day.

I didn't tell my parents. I figured I just had a bad cold. Then I had a second episode. This time I told them. We went right to the family doctor.

My symptoms indicated asthma, he said, and tested me for allergies that might have triggered it. I had plenty: pollen, dust, mold spores. Worse, I was sensitive to chlorine. "Some kids grow out of asthma," he said, handing me a generic "rescue" inhaler. "Use this if you feel tight. Call me if it doesn't help."

My asthma didn't interfere with my training. Good thing, since my schedule was pretty intense. Up at 4:30 a.m. In the pool at American University in Washington, D.C., from 5 a.m. till 7 a.m. On to middle school in Arlington, Virginia. Back again to American to train from 3:30 p.m. till 6 p.m. One day, breaststroke; the next day, freestyle; the following day, butterfly; the next day, backstroke. Individual medley swimmers have to be good at them all. Seven days a week, an average of 15,000 yards a day. I was winning a lot of meets, making a name for myself. At fifteen, I swam the U.S. Junior National Championships. I finished first in the 400-meter individual medley. I have a chance to do something really special, I realized.

I was excited about starting college at the University of Michigan. Coach Jon Urbanchek is internationally known for developing top IM swimmers, and the team had three of the top five IM swimmers in the world. One was Eric.

But my workouts were off, right from the start of freshman year. I was losing weight, getting sick a lot. My dorm room was on the first floor. That fall, every time I opened the window, dust and crumbling leaves flew in. My allergies were worse than ever. But I kept showing up for practice. Finally, Coach sent me to an asthma and allergy specialist.

Terrible news.

"Not only do you have allergic asthma, you have exercise-induced asthma too," he said. "The more intense your workouts, the worse your condition could get."

Intense? That was an understatement. Heck, my eyes were on the Olympics! I went to a specialist who discovered my windpipe was much narrower than normal, something I'd been born with. He put me on a series of inhalers. For the first time, I had an individual program designed specifically to manage my asthma.

Even so, the medications couldn't keep up with my training regimen. If I cut back, I'd never stay on top of the competition. Sometimes I had to wonder: How could a top swimmer be so unlucky as to end up with asthma?

My sophomore year, as a kind of bonus, the team flew to Hawaii for two weeks away from frosty Michigan, just to work out. We practiced in a prep school pool. I was in the water, racing the other guys. Midway through the race, my chest grew tight. It felt as if someone had wrapped a belt around me and was squeezing as hard as possible. I tried to take a breath. Hardly any air came in. Keep swimming. I'd gutted through this sort of thing before. This time it was just too hard. I dragged myself out of the water.

Coach crouched on the pool apron, holding out my inhaler. I took a puff. Then another. Too late. My lungs wouldn't open. My head swam. I turned to Coach. "I'm seeing black spots," I gasped.

That was the last thing I remember. I came around in the emergency room, breathing in medicine through a mask. "With asthma as severe as yours," the doctor said, "this kind of episode is bound to happen again. You need to monitor your condition more carefully if you want to keep swimming." I couldn't help hearing the skeptical emphasis he put on that "if." If. I had a choice—to fight back or give up. Really, it was no choice. If I lived my life worrying about what could go wrong, I'd never accomplish a thing. We all have strengths and weaknesses, I thought. I have to live the life that God gave me.

The next day I was back in the pool, training with a new ferocity, monitoring my asthma closer than ever. That was the key—treating asthma as seriously as competitive swimming. In the year leading up to the 1996 Olympics, I kept my world record in the 400-meter IM.

Now I stood on the starting block in Atlanta, readying to swim for the gold. I felt confident. All at once it hit me: I wouldn't be half the competitor I was had I not had to battle asthma. These other guys have no idea how determined I am, I thought. I've got a real edge on them.

The starting horn sounded. The eight of us hit the water. My family and friends screamed from the stands. Eric and I pulled away early. We were neck and neck. With fifty meters to go, Eric led by three-one-hundredths of a second—the tip of a finger. I was only fifty meters from my goal of taking what God had given me and winning with it. Nobody is going to beat you, I told myself.

I churned the water, straining for the finish line. Soon as I touched the pool wall, I looked up at the electronic scoreboard. I had beaten Eric by thirty-five-hundredths of a second. I'd won the gold.

Later, a reporter asked me, "How many more medals could you have won if you didn't have asthma?"

"Maybe I wouldn't have won any," I told him. "Maybe I wouldn't have known how to overcome adversity." I wouldn't have known what I had in me, what we're all given—the ability to overcome a weakness, to turn it into a strength.

Firestorm
at Our Back Door

SHARON DRYDEN

Driving home from the farmers market in Truckee that hot, windy August afternoon on winding Highway 89 through the Tahoe National Forest, a friend and I were startled to see a tree in flames at a campground along the road. We were in the midst of a dry summer, and any fire in the forest had the potential of becoming dangerous. A U.S. Forest Service worker was standing there with a shovel, looking up at the burning tree. It was not a good sign.

By the time I arrived home a half hour later, my husband, Forest, was running down the driveway, pulling on his volunteer fireman's yellow turnout coat. "There's a fire!" he shouted as he jumped into his pickup.

"I know," I called. "I just saw it."

I watched him disappear down the long residential block on his way to the firehouse, and my stomach fluttered. Although the fire was about fifteen miles away, anything could happen on a day like this.

Suddenly I smelled it. Smoke! I craned my neck to see past our white two-story home and the skyscraper pines that framed it. A plume of gray smoke ominously wafted over the mountainside just beyond the golden meadow behind our home. Many ridges sat between the flames and our house, but southwesterly winds were whipping the fire right toward us.

As the Loyalton-Sierra–Brooks fire engine screamed down the road, an alarm of fear sounded in me as well. I tried to pray away my panic, but it still crept into me, like the smoke sneaking over our mountains.

Within hours a smoky, acrid haze pervaded our mile-high valley, so that even home was no longer a haven. Fire trucks streamed in from surrounding counties. News flashes reported that twenty-five-mile-per-hour winds and dry timber were feeding the fire. A numbness washed over me. A firestorm could be raging at our back door in hours.

I hurriedly threw photos and clothing into suitcases, then commandeered our kids—Crystal, fifteen, Matthew, thirteen, and Alayna, seven. They grabbed our two cats, calico Calle and all-black Domino, and our border collie, Panda. We all jumped into my in-laws' old motor home stored in our driveway, and in minutes we were headed to my sister Denise's home in Reno, forty miles away. I had to escape; I could not fight another battle.

We had already been through so much in the past few

years. First Forest had required surgery for a collapsed lung. Our medical insurance company went defunct, nearly bankrupting us. Next, Matthew almost died from leukemia. Exhausted from the financial and emotional toll, I had struggled through anxiety and depression, until we moved into our new home in Sierra Brooks, a rural subdivision four miles north of Loyalton. It was, I felt, a symbol from God: a better life was ahead for us.

In the Sierra we explored streams and mountain paths, discovering flora and wildlife. I loved our dream house, which we had built ourselves—a split-level with vaulted interior ceilings and muted gray-and-pastel furnishings.

But now I feared yet another trial. *It's too much, God,* I prayed. *Please make the fire go away.*

It didn't. The next morning Forest called to tell me the Cottonwood Fire, as it had been named, was roaring toward our home. "Get our stuff," he said, "the fire's coming." Suddenly I began to quiver. Too shaky to drive, I asked Denise to take me back to our subdivision. When we got there, she had to inch her car around road blockades. Fire trucks guarded every other house, and heat hung in the air.

Three firemen met us at my home and readied it for a fiery battle. They covered windows with blankets, guided our 4-H pig to a trailer, and removed the gas barbecue and woodpile from the fire-facing backyard.

Trying to review my mental lists, I gathered the most important things of our lives. There's money in an envelope, Forest had said. Get Crystal's saddle. Matthew's new air rifle. Alayna's—what did Alayna want? Toys?

The firemen helped me with it all—the computer, photo albums, my wedding dress, Grandma's cookie jar, the children's guardian-angel pictures. My brown Jeep Wagoneer looked like a Dust Bowl migrant family's jalopy stuffed with our most important earthly possessions.

Seeing the panic in my eyes, a friend, Brad, walked up and put his arm around me. A veteran U.S. Forest Service fire manager, he was the commander for the western edge of the fire. "We'll do the best we can, Sharon," he said.

I knew he would: the orange-red firestorm—more than 27,000 acres in size—was already cresting the western mountainside, threatening his nearby home as well. The heat pushed me in waves, and as I tried to swallow, I tasted soot. I watched the fire hungrily lick its way over the mountain. My heart was pounding. I knew then I was probably seeing my home for the last time.

Back at my sister's home in Reno, exhaustion hit me. Frightened as I was, I hadn't cried yet. I felt I had to hold myself together for the sake of the kids. Grungy and reeking of smoke, I headed for the shower, where my tears fell with the soothing streams.

"God, I can't take it anymore. I haven't seen Forest these two days—just two quick calls. Is he okay? And my home may already be gone. Why would You give me a home, a sanctuary, then take it away? I'm so afraid."

I let the water run over me, remembering the last time I had to trust God in a big way. Matthew had been almost four when he was dying from leukemia. At a nurse's prompting, I sought out the hospital's chapel. There I had prayed, "I love Matthew, Lord, and I want him to live. But He's yours, and I give him back to You."

It hadn't been an attempt to bargain with God. I had given up my son because I knew God wanted my surrender and trust most of all. And soon Matthew was on the road to healing and complete remission.

Now I prayed in the shower, "Lord, You have faithfully brought us through each hardship. Why should You not be trustworthy again?"

I sighed. I would still trust God for everything in my life. There would be no trying to bargain. As the water soothed my aching body, He calmed my soul. I knew then that no matter what the outcome of the Cottonwood Fire, God would take care of all of us.

Just minutes after my shower my husband's sister telephoned. "The fire's on the six o'clock news, Sharon. Go watch it."

Grimly I sat on the couch. The kids were still outside playing. Denise was at the grocery store. Trying to hold back tears, I rested my face in my hands and watched the TV.

A white-haired reporter in a yellow firefighter's shirt was reporting live. My neighborhood stood in the background; smoke billowed through the pines on the hills behind the houses.

Then suddenly the scene changed and I saw it. Our home! The front of the house filled the television screen. I held my breath as the shots changed every few seconds . . . the firestorm rushing toward our house . . . flames swallowing hundred-foot trees in a moment . . . Brad lighting a backfire at the edge of our yard . . . one of our trees bursting into flames, just feet from the house . . . a fireman spraying foam over the kids' swing set . . . a helicopter dropping water from a bucket.

What happened then so shocked me that I wasn't sure I was seeing what I thought I saw. A sudden force of wind blew back the massive wall of flames—and in an instant the firestorm switched its course! Instead of heading toward our home, it turned almost completely around and rushed south. I gasped as the reporter confirmed that the fire had not damaged a single house. "Oh, thank You, God . . . thank You!" I almost shouted.

It was several days until things returned to normal. Another arm of the fire continued to threaten nearby Loyalton for two days. The population tripled in size during that week, as more than 2,500 firefighters from the Forest Service and California Department of Forestry and volunteers from all over the West converged on our town of 1,200. Schools, the city park, and surrounding alfalfa fields looked like war encampments.

Finally, the fire burned itself out near the Nevada border north of Reno. More than 48,600 acres of Tahoe National Forest and grazing land were consumed by the Cottonwood Fire of 1994. But not a home was lost—not a life. Some say the backfire helped switch the fire's direction, saving the houses. But even the fire manager in charge, Brad, said it was a miracle.

The next afternoon I returned home alone. As I pulled into the driveway, I noticed a television news team interviewing a group of firefighters. I timidly approached and gasped when I saw Forest standing with them. I had almost not recognized him. He was covered with soot, his thick brown hair was rumpled, and exhaustion was etched into his face. And his boots! The soles had been melted away! The intensity of the danger hit me, and I fell into his arms.

News reporters moved toward us. One newswoman—twentyish, dressed in jeans, perky in the midst of us battle-weary locals—brushed aside her layered brown hair. "Ma'am," she said, "I bet you feel really lucky." She smiled sympathetically as she poised her pencil over her notepad.

I looked at her in disbelief. As the news camera

zoomed in, I shook my head and measured my words. "Lucky," I said, "is finding a penny. This has nothing to do with luck."

And as I walked back to our home with my arm around my husband and his around me, I thanked God. For He had shown me once again that when I put my faith completely in Him, He takes care of my needs more wonderfully than I can even ask. He is worthy of my trust—every time—even in the toughest times.

Harvest of Faith

JUANITA BUSCHKOETTER

When Darrel and I got married in 1985 in a little church in Lawrence, Nebraska, we weren't just marrying each other. We were marrying ourselves to a dream, a dream of running a small family farm in the heartland of America, as Darrel's folks had done for generations. We weren't fools. We knew farming was tough these days for the little guy, almost impossible sometimes. But we had faith. Faith in our love, in our dream, and in God. We thought nothing was impossible.

I met Darrel when I was sixteen. He was twenty-two and more serious than the boys I knew. We sat on the tailgate of his cherry-red Chevy pickup, swinging our legs and talking. Darrel was already renting a 900-acre farm. His eyes lit up when he talked about working the land, watching the tidy rows of seeds he planted sprout, breathing air tinged with the scent of freshly mowed hay. He made farming sound so romantic to a town girl like me. He invited me to visit, and I nearly swooned.

When I drove up to Darrel's place he greeted me at his front door, holding two spade shovels. "I need to get rid of the musk thistles in the grazing pasture," he explained. "Wanna help?"

"Sure," I said, having no idea what he was talking about. He handed me a shovel. I followed Darrel's lead as he started digging out the purple-flowered stalks. It was hot, sweaty work, but later when I looked out at the cleared green pasture I felt a tremendous sense of accomplishment. This is why he's so passionate about farming.

From then on, after his day's work was done, Darrel came into town to see me. Sometimes he was so tired he fell asleep while we were talking. I didn't mind. It was wonderful just to be with him. What I loved most were our dates on his farm. I never felt closer to Darrel than when we worked side by side in the fields.

One evening a year after we started courting, we were sitting on his truck's tailgate under a sky sprinkled with stars. Darrel looked at me and said, "Juanita, I want to spend the rest of my life with you."

My mother was shocked when I told her we wanted to get married as soon as I graduated. My older brothers and sisters had gone on to college, and my parents had expected me to do the same. "Are you sure you understand what you're getting yourself into?" Mom asked. "Farmers have a hard life. So do their wives. And you're so young." The way I saw it, Darrel and I could get through anything together.

It's customary around here to get pearled before you get engaged. Darrel promised he'd go into town at first spring rainfall to buy me a pearl ring. "Can't do any planting when it rains," he explained. I should have realized then the farm would come before everything in our life.

A year after our wedding Audrey was born. The harvest came in fine too that year. We had Abby in '87. I looked after the girls while Darrel worked the wheat, milo, corn, and alfalfa fields. We also had about forty-five cows and farrowed about 100 sows, and it was my job to take care of the newborn pigs. I worked hard, harder than I ever had, but life was good. Our dream was becoming reality.

Maybe that's what burst our bubble—reality. Drought hit central Nebraska in '88. Day after day I scanned the horizon, praying for a rain cloud. Our fields of grain went dry as kindling. At least we had the livestock. But when we took the hogs to the sale barn we barely got enough to pay the feed bills. "It's a bad year for everyone," Darrel said, trying to be philosophical. "It happens."

We were behind in our payments to seed, fuel, and fertilizer suppliers. "Don't worry," Darrel told me. "When the crop comes in next year, we'll get out of the hole." But another drought hit. I asked God why the dream I believed He had put in our life was turning into a nightmare.

In early 1991 our daughter Whitney was born. By December the bank was ready to liquidate our farm. Darrel swallowed his pride and found a six-dollar-an-hour factory job in town. I applied for a restructuring loan with the Farm Service Agency. "They can't turn us down!" Darrel said, angry at having to ask. "We did everything in our power for a good harvest."

But the loan administrator said it would take some time before they came to a decision. I wanted to scream. So much of what was happening was out of our control! We had to take matters into our own hands. I wrote a letter to our senator, begging for his help. When Darrel came home from the factory, he scarfed down dinner, then headed out to the fields. Most nights he didn't come to bed until 2:00 a.m. I felt as though I were raising the children alone, and I worried what it was doing to them. I felt alone, period.

Still the farm cost us more than it made. Like so many small farmers we were drowning in debt, unable to make ends meet no matter how much we worked and sacrificed. I told Darrel, "I'm going to start cleaning houses. I don't see how else we can make it."

He stared at his dusty boots. There was a long silence between us, a deadness in the air married people come to dread. I found myself thinking, *Mom was right. This dream is destroying us.* Without answering, Darrel went back out to the barn.

Darrel's every spare waking moment was consumed by the farm. "Do you think we could spend some time together as a family?" I demanded one evening.

"I need to get back to the fields." He walked out the door.

In February 1993 our loan finally came through. Darrel started the spring planting. I took a college correspondence course to learn more about business agriculture. Even with both of us working outside jobs, we were barely scraping by. It was impossible to clothe and feed three kids on $11,000 a year. I gave in and applied for food stamps. It was more than my husband's shredded pride could withstand.

"We don't take handouts," he shouted when I told him. "We can make do on our own."

"Well, we haven't been," I fired back. "I'm tired of feeding the girls macaroni and cheese all the time, tired of buying them secondhand clothes. They deserve better."

Darrell was so angry he stalked off without another word.

After that, the tension between us mounted. We went about our work, barely speaking to each other, Darrel's anger forcing me further and further away. "Look what's happening to us," I said one night. "We need to talk."

"That's the last thing I want to do. I'm beat," was all Darrel said before falling asleep.

"Lord," I moaned, "what are we going to do? We can't go on like this."

At church every Sunday I told God He had to save

our farm. He had to save our marriage, our dream. *Remember, Juanita,* I said to myself, *faith is what you have when you don't have anything left.* After services one Sunday our priest, Father Au, took me aside. "I'm worried about you and Darrel," he said.

I'd been a Sunday regular through thick and thin, but I'd never asked my church family for help. It was so hard to admit we weren't making it.

"We're struggling," I owned up. "Really struggling, and it's not just the farm." Then everything about our troubles spilled out, like a terrible pressure that had to be relieved.

"There's a good marriage retreat I know of," Father Au said. "Why don't you and your husband consider it?"

I wanted desperately to go. To my relief Darrel agreed without much fuss, and I found myself thinking back to that night on the tailgate of his pickup when he said he wanted to spend the rest of his life with me. He still wants this marriage to work, but does he want it more than the farm?

The retreat helped. We also went into counseling, but it didn't fix all our problems instantly. One night I admitted, "Deep down I guess I do partially blame you for our circumstances, Darrel. I probably trusted you to make this work too much. Maybe I shouldn't have been so naive."

My husband's eyes misted and he looked away. Darrel

is not a man who gives in easily to tears. "I know I put a lot of pressure on you," he said. "I'm sorry. I just want the farm to work, for us. It's why we're together."

"No, Darrel, we're not together because of the farm. We're together because of us. We have to put us and the girls ahead of the farm, and God in front of everything. It's His plan, not ours. We forgot that."

I reached for his hand, and for the first time in a long while, we prayed together. It was a good start, but there was a lot of damage to repair.

"I don't want to clean houses for the rest of my life," I told Darrel one day. "I need to go to school so I can get a better job." He feared I would become fed up with farming life and leave. "Nothing could be further from my mind," I told him. "This will mean a better life for us. You'll be able to quit the factory." Darrel relented. I received a grant and started taking part-time classes toward an associate's degree in ag business.

We continued counseling and we continued battling our money problems and, from time to time, each other. Again and again Darrel's anger boiled up between us. But the '96 spring planting went well. By fall our farm was brimming with sturdy stalks of corn and wheat. Still there was tension. One afternoon I packed sandwiches and a pitcher of iced tea for Darrel and me, and we took a ride into the heart of the fields to inspect our harvest.

In the cab of the pickup Darrel added up the bounty

on his pocket calculator. "We've been waiting for years for this," he exulted. "We'll be able to pay our bills finally."

Yet the anger that Darrel had stored up during all those years of uncertainty was proving a lot harder to get rid of than our debts. Sometimes he would lose control to the point where it scared me. "I can't stay around for any more battles," I told him. "I love you, but if you want things to work out, you have to learn how to manage your anger."

"I'll do anything to keep us together," Darrel said. "Nothing is more important to me, not even this farm." Then he put his arms around me and we held each other for a long time.

So Darrel went to an anger counseling group. He said it had finally sunk in that it takes a strong man to ask for help. "It's one thing to pray," he explained. "But sometimes the Lord wants you to follow up with action. That's the tough part."

Our roles shifted. I continued my college courses while Darrel became the stay-at-home parent, picking the girls up from school and lending a hand around the house in addition to working the farm. "The farm won't matter," he told me, "if I don't have you and the girls."

When I stepped up to get my diploma two summers ago you never saw a prouder person than Darrel. I landed a good job with a local farm insurance company, helping other farmers like us realize their dreams.

I believe the hardest times are behind us, and not just because the farm is doing better. That can change in the blink of an eye. We're doing better—Darrel, the girls, and me. Never again will our family face adversity without God in front of our lives, leading the way. Our dream has taken us on a journey in faith, a journey that goes far beyond what we'd first imagined—coaxing a harvest from a sometimes unyielding land. We've learned we, too, have been planted on this earth and nurtured by God to grow in ways we could never imagine.

Chemo Hair

SUSAN FARR FAHNCKE

W hat are you doing?" The last thing I expected (or wanted) to see was my little sister, lying sideways across the guest bed in our house, calmly running her fingers through her "chemo hair" and dropping the handfuls of beautiful silky blonde hair into the wastebasket next to the bed.

My gorgeous twenty-eight-year-old sister was losing her battle with brain cancer and accepted it with a grace and gratitude that at times blew me away. Like now.

Angel had always been very "into" her looks. I'm sure it stemmed from losing her hair at the age of three from her first battle with cancer. She beat that one, but when her hair came back, it was always very thin. Her entire life, she had fretted about her hair, sensitive to its never being quite as thick as she'd like. This past year it had grown to her shoulders and was a shiny, silky blonde that framed her pretty face just right. Now her face looked battle-ravaged—bruised from constantly losing her balance (a side effect of the brain tumor), swollen from the steroids that she needed to help keep her brain from swelling. I never understood how the steroids could differentiate between the swelling in her brain and the swelling in her face. How did they diminish one and cause the other? Her hair was no longer framing her lovely face; it was now simply falling out around her.

"What are you DOING?" I asked again. A little half-smile lit her face.

"I'm thanking God." Her words will forever stay with me. My baby sis taught me every single day of her life since her brain cancer diagnosis. She could see the blessing in every single situation, no matter how desperately they frightened me. I laughed at her upside-down pose, hanging off the bed, pulling the rest of her hair out and dropping it like it was nothing more than a disposable afterthought. I didn't know whether she was losing her marbles along with her hair, or was serious about thanking God as she lost her crowning glory.

"What are you thanking Him for?" I was puzzled, but knew there was a lesson here. I just had to wait for it.

"Because I have a chance to grow thick hair now!" She seemed surprised at my stupidity. "I've always hated my hair, and now it's falling out, I can grow new hair."

Most women I know, including myself, would be a LOT more upset—hysterically crying, actually, at being faced with losing their hair on top of everything else a cancer patient has to endure. For women, your hair is a huge part of your identity. In fact, I personally have always been known BY my hair. I'm a redhead and have spent my whole life being called "red," "carrot top," "that redhead" . . . I don't think I'd know who I am without my hair. But here was my sister, with an almost Zen-like acceptance of this new phase in her life, not only not hysterical, but feeling thankful! She always taught me that no matter how bad things seemed, how heart-wrenching and gut-deep our pain was, there was always something to be thankful for.

She has been gone six years now. It's hard to believe it's been that long. In many ways, I feel like she was just with me yesterday. Things she did or said or taught me continually come back to me, often out of the blue. Her spirit of gratitude and joy in life were beautiful gifts that continue to bless me, even after all this time.

On days when I'm having a bad hair day or feel cranky because of something superficial, I find myself remembering her thanking God on what could have been one of the lowest days of her life. Instead of going into a tailspin and feeling lost without her locks, she simply found the hope that comes with change, and truly, from the deepest part of her heart, felt grateful for it.

Angel's hair never did quite come in much, but the greatest changes possible in a person's life did flow forth and would never have done so without her battle with cancer. She became a brilliant example of what God wants us to become during our time on earth. She learned there is a rainbow within every cloud and that there is always something to be thankful for.

On this day, a day, when you might feel less than grateful for life's hardships and challenges, remember a beautiful twenty-eight-year-old woman, her golden hair falling out, and thanking God for it. There is always something for which to be thankful.

CHAPTER 4

W aiting for the Sunrise

Crying may last for a night, but joy comes in the morning.
(Psalm 30:5)

Have you ever had one of those nights when you just can't get to sleep? Or perhaps you awaken in the middle of the night and can't go back to sleep? You're restless. Frustrated. You have something on your mind that's disturbing your peace of mind, and sleep just won't come. Perhaps you're going through a tough time in your life—health, family, finances. So you spend the night tossing and turning, waiting for the sunrise. And somehow, when the sun does finally rise and chase away the darkness, the fears and worries of the night fade away too. Life always looks better in the light of day, doesn't it?

To Live Again

NANETTE THORSEN-SNIPES

The rain slid down my windshield in rivulets and everything seemed blurry as I wiped away tears. The tractor-trailer had roared past me a half hour before, kicking up water as it sped by. I looked at my still trembling hands. They were red where I'd gripped the steering wheel. At once, I realized how close I had come to pulling in front of the truck.

"God," I whispered, "please help me." I had never felt so alone in my life. Even though I was married with four children, a cat, and a dog, I felt completely alone. And empty.

I stopped living—really living—on the Saturday after Thanksgiving in 1983. My second husband, Jim, and I had made an early morning grocery run. We'd just gotten back when my strapping fifteen-year-old son stopped me cold. His brown eyes were filled with pain. He tried to talk, but the words lodged in his throat.

"What's wrong?" I screamed. I shook his shoulders in desperation. Frightening words tumbled out. "Dad killed himself," he said.

No! I thought, *It can't be true.* My former husband was still young. At forty, he had built another life with his second wife; he owned a beautiful house, had a good job—everything he could ask for. No, it was a horrible mistake.

"Mom," my son said, "did you hear me?"

Memories seared my mind and somewhere in the recesses, I wondered, *Why?* I recalled the long-ago spring day in my bedroom with my lavender curtains fluttering in the breeze. I sat on the edge of the bed as my husband tossed clothes into a suitcase after I'd said I wanted a separation. I needed peace in my life as the endless battles had exhausted me. I had wanted a separation because his anger and hostility terrified me.

While packing his clothes, he asked a question that chilled me. "You're really going to do it, aren't you? You're really going to leave."

A small voice I barely recognized as mine said yes.

I was horrified to see him walk to the closet shelf and pull down the large black gun we'd bought for protection. He began inserting bullets into each chamber. I heard each one click and measured my life in each one.

Tears dripped off my chin as the memory faded and the reality of his death set in. *Why?* The assurance of Jim's arm around me added comfort and softened the news. Memories of my former roller-coaster marriage faded into the past. My mind couldn't contain the pain.

How could he do this? How could he leave his children?
As one year turned into nine, the anger consumed me.
Soon, I found myself unable to concentrate. I couldn't
remember to keep dentist or doctor appointments, names
vanished, and I couldn't follow a simple recipe. Doing my
laundry, if I could remember, was a huge task.

Once, Jim insisted I go to a family reunion, but I
couldn't. It was more than I could handle. It took every
ounce of strength just to make it to the next day.

"I can't go," I said softly.

"Sure you can," he said, encouraging me.

I began screaming inside. *I can't go. Don't you understand? Aren't you listening?* In minutes, the rage I'd bottled
up for years, exploded, and I began weeping uncontrol-
lably.

"I think you'd better see a counselor," he said.

I shook my head, wiping away tears with the back of
my hand. "I'll be all right."

This last emotional event brought me to the side of
the road a week later. As I crossed over the expressway
on my way home from the doctor's office, I saw a tractor-
trailer bearing down on me. *It would be so easy. It would
be over in just a few moments. All I had to do was swerve
in front of the truck.*

The truck rumbled toward my car, its back wheels
kicking up water. I gripped the steering wheel. *All I had
to do was pull into its path.* My breath caught in my

throat. As I allowed the truck to pass, it rattled my car. I pulled over. *What is wrong with me?* I put my car in park with the motor still running.

I watched a lightning bolt arc across the sky and the clouds crack open. Raindrops pelted my windshield. I let the tears flow.

"God," I prayed, "please help me."

I sat there for what seemed an eternity. As the rain slowed, I saw sunshine slicing through the clouds. A beginning peace began in my heart, and I could almost feel an inner voice remind me, *My grace is sufficient for you, for my power is made perfect in weakness.*

As the biblical message sank in, I knew what had to be done. With my newfound strength, I called a Christian counselor. After several years of counseling, I was relieved to know that my thoughts of suicide were merely a cry for help.

One day after I had begun rising early for devotions, I read in the Bible that I was a child of God, and He loved me very much. I could barely fathom such love, but on a human level that was how much my husband loved me.

Jim loved me enough to stand by me as I dealt with the loss of my former husband. He went with me to counseling week after week, sharing my pain and anguish. He even offered to go with me to the gravesite to say a final good-bye—a moment of forgiving, of releasing the anger inside. The pain was so great that I never made it physically to his grave. However, I later imagined standing in front of his headstone and saying once and forever, "I'm sorry, Benny."

Sometime later, I was up at daybreak to watch the sun rise. I poured coffee and walked to my back porch swing. Warming my hands on the mug, I marveled at the first rays of light. I sat there a long time, wondering what had happened to the years the locusts had eaten.

Unlike the rainy day I sat in my car trembling, I was alive for the first time in years. I watched vibrant colors of lavender and pink filter across the sky as the sun blinked above the horizon. The back door groaned open, and I shared the day's beauty with Jim as he sat down beside me.

He put his arm around me and gently squeezed my shoulder. I felt the soft touch of a breeze playing in my hair.

My grace is sufficient for you. My heart leapt with joy at the closeness of the Lord's presence.

I closed my eyes, and I thanked Him.

Then Came the Flood

CAROL GREEN

We sat in the dark in my sister's living room, the six of us, and listened to the telltale cracks of trees splitting, the constant lashing of rain against the windows, the house groaning as water and mud rose to the sills outside. No one said a word. We had vowed to stay together through the night—me and my husband, Nate; my sister, Bonnie, and her husband; my mother and my father. Plus our two dachshunds, Freddy and Minnie. All of us waiting for our lives to be washed away with the house and the ranch. After all, if we lost the ranch, what good were our lives?

Establishing the ranch had been everything for our family. My mother and father had spent more than fifty backbreaking years carving the place out of a dry and desolate corner of northeastern California. They built the ranch house a quarter mile from the hillside, not far from a stream we used for irrigation. In the corral below we'd raised a dairy barn, a separator house (where we separated cream from milk), a hay barn, the tack shed, and oil shed. We kids grew up on that land, married and set up households of our own. I settled nearby with my husband and continued to work the ranch.

We mended fences, drove cattle to the summer ranges, brought them home in the fall. We were never far from the smell of horses, dampened leather, dust, sage, and juniper. It was hard, honest work—cowboy work, I guess—but I wouldn't have traded it for the highest-paying city job. This was God's country, and we lived close to it, and close to Him.

Then came the flood.

On New Year's Day 1997, Nate and I went with my father to help feed the cattle. It had rained almost every day for two weeks straight, sometimes a mist, sometimes a heavy rain falling onto snowpack in the mountains. The field was a muddy mess, and the stream behind my parents' house was running high and fast, transformed from a gentle brook to a raging river.

We spent a long hour trying to channel the flow away from the house, but couldn't do it. We called a neighbor who brought his backhoe. The water kept coming. Other neighbors helped, but by early afternoon their ranches were flooding too. We fixed our neighbors' dinner before they rushed home. Afterward I was at the back porch, washing up, when I saw a dark avalanche of mud and debris rushing toward the house.

"Grab the dogs and go out the front!" I hollered.

Dad pulled the back door shut and each of us drove

in car, truck, or tractor to Bonnie's house, a quarter mile away.

There we settled down to rest, but nothing could induce me to sleep. Like a caged cat, I paced. Finally I lay down, but then a horrid, stomach-churning boom rattled the house from top to bottom. All the lights went out. I got up and put on my clothes.

"It was just the rain and wind," Nate said.

"Ain't no wind sound like that," my mother declared. Bonnie lit an old coal-oil lantern, and we phoned 911 to tell them where we were. They couldn't send anyone to get us in the dark, so my husband assured them we'd be fine riding out the storm together. Dad was silent, his jaw set. I think he knew before the rest of us how little hope was left.

With the coal-oil lamp Bonnie and I went out to the back porch to see what had hit us. All at once another slip of mud and debris came roaring down the hill like a runaway train. An uprooted tree hurtled toward us. "Carol! Shut that door!" my sister screamed. I slammed the kitchen door just as a thirty-foot-long tree trunk smashed it hard.

Bonnie went around to the front. "I smell gas," she cried. Sure enough, the line was broken. I blew out the coal-oil lamp. Now there was no heat, no light. We had one flashlight with weak batteries, but we decided to save it for when we really needed it. There in the pitch dark of the living room we waited, nobody saying a word. We paced the room and listened to the rain and wind groaning outside the house. Just waiting.

So is this what it comes to? I wondered. Was this what came from living so close to God's earth and making a life for ourselves? All the years of toil and sweat wiped out in a matter of minutes? *Lord, keep us safe.* In my anguish I could barely pray, but I forced myself. I could not allow my despair to separate me from the only resource we had left. There was my father, my mother, my sister, brother-in-law, and husband. What would we have left without the ranch?

A little past midnight a log broke through a window. My sister kept a sheet of plywood under her bed for her back, so we put that over the window. "We have to look for higher ground!" I shouted.

My father shook his head. He wasn't going anywhere. He would rather die than leave the ranch.

"No," we implored him. "Come with us."

Finally we coaxed him to the bedroom, where we helped one another through the window. It was dark. The rain poured down like I couldn't believe. We slogged across the yard to the old wash shed behind the house, stopping to take in the scene.

A huge log wedged precariously between the shed and the house was the only thing that had kept us from washing away in the path of the slips. The wood shed had been tipped over and all the buildings below it were gone. My father's car had been smashed into a jumbled mass with the old pickup, and the whole of our land as far as we could see had turned into mud and water.

My father looked at my husband. "You think there's any way you can get out?"

Nate shook the rain from his hat. "I'd be a fool to even try."

When we saw how the log had blocked the water, and saw the water and debris behind it, when we felt the wind and rain, we reasoned we would be better off back in the house. "If that log gives," I said, "we'll be gone too."

One by one we climbed back into the house. The phone was still working, so I called a neighbor to say where we were and how many of us there were. If rescuers ever came, I wanted them to know. My brother-in-law kept getting up from the couch to fix himself soda water because he had an upset stomach. My father, breathing heavily, rested in a rocker by the door. My sister and I paced the floor.

My father thought he heard engines rumbling. "Here they come for us," he called out. "Here they are!"

Our hearts raced with hope. Nate climbed out the bedroom window, but could see nothing. He worked his way to the tractor and took it down the field, but he couldn't reach the road.

When he came back he told us, "I'm only going to

say this once, because I can't believe it myself. There's nothing left. The ranch is gone."

At first light Nate and my brother-in-law went out, and that time they got the tractor to the highway, where they met our rescuers. EMTs and firemen had hit mud in the road about a quarter mile away, stopped their vehicles, and come across on foot through the mud, fifteen feet deep in places.

I took a few things and stuffed them in a pillowcase. With the pillowcase slung over my back and one of the dachshunds under my arm, I started to the road. A quarter mile through heavy mud, one step at a time. I sank until something stopped me. Sometimes I sank five inches and kept walking. Other times I sank to my hip, and had to set the dog down and pull myself out before I could get moving again.

"Don't bring anyone this way," I told the EMTs, "because they won't make it." I went south and the others were hauled out in a tractor and a wagon. Tired, covered in mud, cold to the bone, we finally met up at the firehouse and slept overnight at a motel.

The flood had raged, but the sun was shining brightly on the snowy peaks the next day as we rode back to the ranch. The air smelled damp and rich. And we were still together, the six of us, together and alive.

But the ranch house was gone, clean washed away. Nate's and my home was gone. The huge barn filled with hay, gone. Our milk house was gone. The gas tanks were gone. The saddle shed with all of our riding tack—my brand-new saddle, my husband's six-month-old custom-made saddle—gone. Everything, gone.

My father's sixteen-foot horse trailer and another pickup were washed onto our stock truck. There was no chicken house. No fences. No dry range land. We found some calves dead in the debris, but most of the cows had found safe ground, thank God. I had driven the saddle horses out of the corral earlier and shut the gate, so they were safe. We rescued my father's stock dog, who was buried up to her neck and barking for her life.

Just two days earlier I had told myself there would be no life, nothing without the ranch. As we stood together surveying the devastation, I felt almost elated. There was one thing left standing: our family, the six of us.

My mother must have felt the same way. "People say they don't know what God looks like," she said to me, tears running down her face, "but I know He has six hands. Two nights ago He must have had a hand on each of our heads. And He kept all six of us safe. With His hand on your head, you're going to be okay, aren't you?"

"Yes," I answered.

"No matter what happens, you're going to be okay, right?"

"Yes, Mother, we are going to be okay."

A Bushel and a Peck

LYN ROCHE

I felt the familiar kiss on my forehead. My eyes opened. I mumbled, "Have a good day," rolled over, and promptly fell back to sleep. The next thing I was conscious of was the "beep-beep" of my husband's car horn as he pulled out of the driveway. I sat straight up with the realization that it was his birthday. I hadn't wished him a happy birthday! *I didn't even get up with him!* I thought with a pang of guilt. *What was wrong with me lately?*

I dragged myself out of bed, bathed, and got ready for work. During the drive to my office I tried to think clearly. *How did I let his special day arrive without making any plans to celebrate?* I reminded myself that we weren't making plans ahead these days.

Three years earlier our lives changed when I became the primary caregiver of my grandmother. She had been living with my parents across the state. With the onset of my father's Alzheimer's disease, two patients were more than my mother could handle. So I suggested that my grandmother move near us. After all, I was the only grandchild, and she and I had always been close. She was my father's mother and my "Gam." She agreed to make the move, and it went well.

But in a short time her poor health necessitated another move for her, this time to a nursing home fifteen miles from us. I felt guilty for not being able to take care of her in my home, and I tried to spend as much time with her as I could. Meanwhile, the strange disease called Alzheimer's took more of its devastating toll on my parents. There were long-distance crises and trips across the state.

We made another family decision: They would also move closer to us. A year after their move it became impossible for my mother to continue caring for Dad at home.

Mom and I painstakingly searched for a care facility with a special Alzheimer's unit. The closest one was two hours away. She visited him once or twice a week, and I saw him once a month. I accumulated vast quantities of personal guilt as I tried to juggle all my family roles of wife, mother, daughter, and granddaughter along with maintaining a full-time job in a busy law firm.

Gam was in her mid-nineties and frail. The nursing home staff called me in often for minor and major emergencies. I saw her growing thinner and weaker. Meanwhile, my dad's world was getting smaller and smaller. His care and dwindling finances were battering my mother. My husband and children got less of my attention. I loved them all, but I felt torn. I wasn't sure I was doing enough for anyone.

That's exactly the state I found myself in on my husband's forty-ninth birthday. It was also an intense and stressful day at work. Early in the afternoon I was able to fit in a call to my mother. She said she had been to see Gam and tried to feed her lunch. Water through a straw was about all she would take. I had hoped to go see her that day, but Mom strongly suggested I wait until the next day to visit her. She told me to spend my husband's birthday with him. A sickening wave of guilt swept over me. Decisions were becoming more and more difficult for me to make on my own.

Ultimately, I decided to prepare a special, yet easy birthday dinner. After work I quickly shopped for all the right ingredients. Driving home I made a mental note to pull some flowers from our yard and put them on the table. Once inside the house I noticed a card on the kitchen counter with my name on it. It contained a cheery greeting followed by a message in my husband's handwriting: "I'm at racquetball. Be home soon. How's Gam doing?" Ouch! A card for me, and it's his birthday! More guilt.

I scrambled to prepare dinner. I plucked hibiscus from our favorite bush and created a simple centerpiece. I even managed to take a bath and redo my hair and makeup before my husband got home. We enjoyed a lovely meal together, but as we were finishing I felt an urge to go to the nursing home. *What was going on?* Couldn't I let myself enjoy a whole evening with my husband anymore? No, it was stronger and deeper than that: something other than just my own thoughts. At that moment there was no indecision. I told my husband I had to go. He said he understood and offered to go with me. But just then the phone rang. He answered it. It was one of the children calling from college to talk to him on his special day. I smiled and shook my head—no, I'd go alone.

I looked back as I was leaving. He was laughing with our daughter. One hand held the cordless phone to his ear, and with the other he was clearing the table. I was leaving him with the dirty dishes on his birthday! He looked up and smiled at me as he leaned over to blow out the candles on the table. I prayed that I was doing the right thing. *Is this urge coming from You, Lord?*

For most of the drive I was behind a slow-moving truck and didn't have a chance to pass it. Indecision set in again. *What was I doing? This is ridiculous. Maybe I should just go home. She'll be asleep by now anyway. What was I going to do—just sit by her bed?* I had never gone to the nursing home late at night without being called. Yet, something told me not to turn around.

I pulled into the parking lot and remembered I'd have to ring the night bell to get into the building.

Through the glass of the front door I saw Gina coming down the hall. She was my favorite nurse. Her grandmother had been my grandmother's roommate. Maybe she will understand my crazy behavior.

She opened the door and looked questioningly at me. "How did you get here so fast? I just asked the desk to call you."

"Why? What happened?" I asked.

"Your grandmother died five minutes ago."

Gina hugged me through both of our tears, and we went to Gam's room. She left me alone, and I held Gam in my arms. I talked to her even though I knew she had already left her worn-out earthly body. I told her I loved her "a bushel and a peck." It was a farewell we had exchanged since my childhood. Her response would have been "and a hug around the neck." We shared this special dialogue only a day ago. The memory was sweet, and a warm peace filled me.

The words to one of my favorite songs became a reality in that seemingly empty room. "Surely the presence of the Lord is in this place. . . . " At that moment I knew everything was okay. I understood that what I had been suffering was the pain of loving deeply and thinking I could personally make everything better for all my loved ones. I had constantly believed I wasn't doing enough because I couldn't change things that were out of my control.

I've never forgotten the strong sense of love I felt in Gam's room that night, or the fact that God got me there. I wasn't with Gam when she died, but God and his angels were. And I believe I arrived just when I was supposed to. I know she heard me tell her how much I loved her, and I felt her love for me.

The beautiful gift of peace I received that night has helped me through many things since then, including my father's death years later. I'm not as hard on myself anymore, and I've learned how to help others who struggle with the special challenges of caregiving.

One extraordinary night, God and my grandmother let me know I was doing the best that I could. They love me the way I need to love myself: "a bushel and a peck and a hug around the neck."

The Sparrow at Starbucks

I t was chilly in Manhattan but warm inside the Starbucks shop on 51st Street and Broadway, just a skip up from Times Square. Early November weather in New York City holds only the slightest hint of the bitter chill of late December and January, but it's enough to send the masses crowding indoors to vie for available space and warmth.

For a musician, it's the most lucrative Starbucks location in the world, I'm told, and consequently, the tips can be substantial if you play your tunes right. Apparently, we were striking all the right chords that night, because our basket was almost overflowing.

It was a fun, low-pressure gig—I was playing keyboard and singing backup for my friend who also added rhythm with an arsenal of percussion instruments. We mostly did pop songs from the '40s to the '90s with a few original tunes thrown in. During our emotional rendition of the classic, "If You Don't Know Me by Now," I noticed a lady sitting in one of the lounge chairs across from me. She was swaying to the beat and singing along.

155

After the tune was over, she approached me. "I apologize for singing along on that song. Did it bother you?" she asked.

"No," I replied. "We love it when the audience joins in. Would you like to sing up front on the next selection?"

To my delight, she accepted my invitation.

"You choose," I said. "What are you in the mood to sing?"

"Well . . . do you know any hymns?"

Hymns? This woman didn't know who she was dealing with. I cut my teeth on hymns. Before I was even born, I was going to church. I gave our guest singer a knowing look. "Name one."

"Oh, I don't know. There are so many good ones. You pick one."

"Okay," I replied. "How about 'His Eye is on the Sparrow'?"

My new friend was silent, her eyes averted. Then she fixed her eyes on mine again and said, "Yeah. Let's do that one."

She slowly nodded her head, put down her purse, straightened her jacket and faced the center of the shop. With my two-bar setup, she began to sing, "Why should I be discouraged?"

The audience of coffee drinkers was transfixed. Even the gurgling noises of the cappuccino machine ceased as the employees stopped what they were doing to listen.

The song rose to its conclusion, "For His eye is on the sparrow, and I know He watches me."

When the last note was sung, the applause crescendoed to a deafening roar that would have rivaled a sold-out crowd at Carnegie Hall. Embarrassed, the woman tried to shout over the din, "Oh, y'all go back to your coffee! I didn't come in here to do a concert! I just came in here to get somethin' to drink, just like you!" But the ovation continued. I embraced my new friend.

"You, my dear, have made my whole year! That was beautiful!"

"Well, it's funny that you picked that particular hymn," she said.

"Why is that?"

"Well . . ." she hesitated again, "that was my daughter's favorite song."

"Really!" I exclaimed.

"Yes," she said, and then grabbed my hands. By this time, the applause had subsided and it was business as usual. "She was sixteen. She died of a brain tumor last week."

I said the first thing that found its way through my stunned silence.

"Are you going to be okay?"

She smiled through tear-filled eyes and squeezed my hands. "I'm gonna be okay. I've just got to keep trusting the Lord and singing His songs, and everything's gonna be just fine." She picked up her bag, gave me her card, and then she was gone.

Was it just a coincidence that we happened to be singing in that particular coffee shop on that particular November night? Coincidence that this wonderful lady just happened to walk into that particular shop? Coincidence that of all the hymns to choose from, I just happened to pick the very hymn that was the favorite of her daughter, who had died just the week before? I refuse to believe it.

God has been arranging encounters in human history since the beginning of time, and it's no stretch for me to imagine that He could reach into a coffee shop in mid-town Manhattan and turn an ordinary gig into a revival. It was a great reminder that if we keep trusting Him and singing His songs, everything's gonna be okay.

How I Stopped Drinking

KAREN B.

F our years ago, in the dreary lull that comes with the New Year, I was battling a familiar foe: depression. I'd gone into town to run a few errands, but the looming gray hills only added to my gloom. I bought beer and put gas in the car. Squeezing the metal handle of the nozzle, I tried not to dwell on the parallel between a car's need for fuel and my dependency on alcohol.

Depression and alcoholism ran in my family. Knowing that my feelings were inherited did little to make them more bearable. It was worse, in fact, to think that I was powerless over how I felt, especially at this time of year when people are supposed to feel hopeful about what's to come. What did the New Year hold for me but more unhappiness?

The pump shut itself off with a thunk, stirring me from my half-attentive state. I screwed the cap on the gas tank, got in my car and started the engine, not really wanting to go back to my empty house and the couch where I found myself sitting and drinking so often that it almost seemed a physical part of me.

Next to the gas station was a country store that catered to tourists. The sign outside proclaimed big markdowns on Christmas items. I pulled into the parking lot.

The store was like most rural tourist stops, crowded with candle holders, quilts, handpainted signs. There were two tables of ornaments. My attention was drawn to several angel figures, about eight inches high, with clay heads, hands, and wings. Their robes were of papier-mâché. One in particular, with flowing auburn hair like my own, seemed to call to me. I reached out and picked her up. All of a sudden the strangest feeling welled up, a feeling of peacefulness and reassurance that momentarily overrode my depression. I glanced at her price tag—too much even at 20 percent off. Putting her back, I started to walk away when the thought struck me, *No. That angel is meant for you.*

I returned to the table and picked up the figure again. Turning her over, I noticed that inside her skirt were the initials KB, same as mine. None of the other angels had any writing on them. "This must be for me, after all," I muttered, pulling out my credit card to pay.

Back home, after putting away the groceries and beer, I decided to place the angel on my living room mantel. I cleared a spot and set her down carefully. At that instant, a powerful thought formed in my mind, completely unbidden: *Please help me stop drinking.*

What was I thinking? I had no concept of myself as

someone who did not drink, and the notion of facing my feelings without the buffer of alcohol was completely unnerving. Almost in defiance of the thought, I cracked open another beer and flopped on the couch, staring up at the angel while I drank.

And I kept drinking as the weeks passed, most nights until I nodded off on the couch or stumbled to bed in a depressive fog. I'd go to work in the morning, alcohol still coursing through my system. I did my work well despite the gruesome daily hangover, but relations with my colleagues deteriorated. "Karen," my boss told me during one confrontation, "it's not your work that's the problem, it's you."

I didn't want to hear it, even though it was looking like this would be another job lost, my fourth in as many years. With my family far away, and no friends to speak of, work was about the only place I interacted with any-one at all. Now that was about to fall apart, and I really didn't care. I couldn't care. About anything.

Lying on the living room couch, I'd sometimes find myself staring up at the angel on the mantelpiece. Why did I bring her here? What was that mystifying calmness I'd felt the first time I held her in my hands? Was God trying to tell me He cared about me or was it just a trick of the mind?

By summer I knew I was losing control. I'd always looked at my drinking through a prism of rationalization.

I told myself that if I held a job and owned a home, my drinking couldn't be that bad. But now, as bills and job woes mounted and the drinking took a greater physical toll, I finally admitted that the alcohol I had used for so many years to take the edge off my depression was making it worse.

One night after work, I was sitting in my usual spot on the couch fighting the feelings of shame and worthlessness that lately seemed to be on the verge of smothering me, when I broke down in deep, spasmodic sobs. I didn't even try to stop. I don't know how long I cried, but at some point I heard myself say, "Please, God, destroy my desire to drink!" Yet the very next night I was back on the couch drinking more desperately than ever.

My prayer seemed to open the floodgates wide. Almost at once my drinking became completely reckless. I abandoned the couch and became careless about drinking and driving. And that was what set the stage for my miracle.

The flashing lights of the state trooper's patrol car were a blue blaze in my rearview mirror that night. I was smart enough, at least, to pull off the road and submit to arrest for drunk driving. The trooper took me to the county jail, where I was given a Breathalyzer test, fingerprinted, photographed, and locked in a cell for six hours to sober up. As clarity returned, the true state of my life was laid bare for me. I realized I was killing myself. I wanted to go home. I wanted to see the angel on my mantel. I wanted to sit on my couch and look at her and think.

I had to give the cab driver a hundred dollars in advance to take me the fifty miles home. I walked in the door, sat down on the couch and looked up at the angel figurine. I'd thought of her all the way home. Now I simply stared and stared until I felt something inside me give. The tears came again, but they were tears of relief. Another one of those powerful thoughts I'd been having since the first of the year took hold, and it was as sure as anything I knew: *Thank God, I don't have to drink anymore.*

In that instant, my life changed, and only the word *miracle* can describe it. I came to the end of a long maze after years of being lost within it. Yet staring at my angel, I understood fully that a higher power had guided me through.

Recovery has been a bumpy road, but my life is full of rewards. Quitting alcohol was just the first step in a series of steps I've taken in the last four years. My job is more satisfying, my health is strong, I have friends. My last performance review at work included "good relations with coworkers" as a strength. One big amazing step I took recently was with a man I met at a hiking club. I felt the same strange powerful draw to him that I had felt in the country store. Now the angel on the mantelpiece has two people to watch over, my husband and me.

God has used many ways to show He loves me, that He's always loved me. But it was a clay figurine with auburn hair, on sale for 20 percent off, that He used to save my life.

Through Eyes
That Could Not See

MARCIA K. LEASER

I first became acquainted with Ethel Wickert when I found out she, too, was a poet. We each had our own way of spreading words on paper. My poems were written for ones who were troubled by life. Many of my poems made people cry. The majority of Ethel's poems were funny. By that I mean she made people laugh. I always felt her writing was the greater gift to the world.

One of my favorite poems she wrote was the one about the time she bought shoes too large.

"They were such a bargain, I couldn't pass them up," she said with a smile. The stanza I liked best, in the poem she wrote about her too-big shoes read:

> The best shoes that I owned,
>   I bought a size bigger than mine.
> With tissue paper in the toes,
>   they looked and fit just fine.

> But once when we went dancing,
> when we twirled around and dipped.
> We had to stop—I lost a shoe—
> my tissue paper slipped.

Then at age eighty-six her eyesight began to fail, due to macular degeneration.

We would share our writing often over the phone, and I bought every book she had gotten printed at a local printer's. I can't remember how many books she told me she'd sold when I asked. But it was a lot.

When I put my poems into a book, I proudly presented her with one. She thanked me but said sadly, "I can't read them, you know." I didn't realize her eyesight had gotten so bad.

"Okay, then," I said. "I'll read them to you." And I did.

For the next four and a half years, I went every Tuesday and read to Ethel. I read everything she'd written . . . everything I'd written . . . and I think everything everyone else had written.

We had so much fun. Once or twice she fell asleep. Once I fell asleep. Sometimes I'd say the wrong word, like the time one of the characters developed diabetes. I accidentally read it as *diarrhea*. We laughed so hard.

I never heard her complain one time about not being able to see clearly. I often thought to myself, *Whew, if that was me . . . the world would know.*

We shared many "little secrets" as she called them. But never were hers derogatory about anyone or anything. Not that she'd had an easy life: in fact, far from it. She raised six children at a time when wringer washers, clotheslines, and many other "old fashioned" things were the norm. A time when microwaves were unheard of, and the news was carried into the homes via a radio.

Even though she worked thirty-eight years at the telephone company, her children never lacked for love and guidance. They, today, display the same honesty and integrity Ethel always displayed throughout her entire ninety-three years.

I worried that her family would resent my taking every Tuesday of their mother's life, but they were as gracious as she was and seemed happy to have me there.

Of course, sometimes things would interfere, such as family vacations, etc. Whoever was busy would just call the other and explain, and we'd meet the following week.

People would say to me, "Oh, that's so nice of you to give up your time to read to Ethel." But they didn't have a clue. It was nice of Ethel to let me read to her. I thought of those days as a special gift from God. I thought of *her* as a special gift from God. She was my oasis along the dusty road of life.

Ethel died early Sunday morning, September 18, 2005. I was fortunate enough to be able to say good-bye to her the day before. I told her she would have to finish the book we were in the middle of reading by herself. She wasn't awake when I told her that, but I know she heard me. When I went to see her at the funeral home, I thought it befitting it was a Tuesday.

My memories of Ethel are broad and deep. They are also important, because not only was our writing different, our lives were as well. I was a complainer and a skeptic. She taught me more than she will ever know as I saw a beautiful world through her eyes that could not see. I no doubt will have to live to be at least ninety-three to learn to see things as she did.

When I told her she'd have to finish the book we were reading at the time of her death by herself, I meant it. And through eyes that are able to see clearly today, if I know Ethel, she has.

In His Perfect Time

CARLA M. ZWAHLEN

I think you are adrenaline deprived," said my niece, while she swept up the flower debris strewn around the floor. We were cleaning up after designing and installing the flowers for my client's three-hundred-guest wedding extravaganza. Adrenaline deprived or whatever it was, I ran on empty. It was a hot early evening in August 2004. This wedding project was the first major job I had accepted since my husband, Werner, lost his heroic battle against esophageal cancer in June of 2003.

Werner's death severed the roots of my life. Like a shocked plant, I barely functioned. To begin the severe work of walking through mind-numbing grief, I needed a quiet refuge. That priceless gift of time came from a prince and princess, who offered me a place of refuge at their secluded ancestral chateau in the heart of France.

My sister manages this French prince's international business affairs. In the winter of 2004, her job required her to travel to his chateau, in order to work on an extended major project. When the prince found out about

Werner's death, he extended a kind and gracious invitation to me to accompany my sister and stay at the chateau for as long as I needed. Because nothing about living in a palace environment was familiar to me, and nothing there existed of the life I shared with Werner, the chateau became my perfect refuge.

The mild winter climate in that French region was also a gift. Almost every day, I walked through formal boxwood gardens and into the solitude of the manicured forest surrounding the chateau. I did not walk alone. I had God's promise to rest in His shadow as we walked through the steps of mourning. I deliberately sought His purpose and plan to help me begin my life again when I returned home to New Hampshire in April. One major decision loomed over the rest. Could I continue to live in the home Werner and I shared for thirty-three years? I should not have worried. On the day I returned to my home God knew best how to handle that decision.

On a warm April afternoon, I walked into my home and burst into tears. Werner would never return to this house, and I could not find or recapture my old life there. That abrupt reality and emotional explosion solidified the impossibility of living in my home without Werner. To help calm me, my daughter-in-law took me aside and gave me a glass of water. As I drank the water, I said, "I can't do this. I can't live here." A few months later, I placed my house on the market. The completion of this huge August wedding project marked the last chapter of living in my home.

Alone in my house later that night I finally sank into a chair. My thoughts roved back over the day's wedding work. Then my thoughts tread on shaky ground. *Werner, you would have been proud of the work we accomplished and how exquisite the flowers looked in the grand ballroom.* I should have known better. His silent voice roared around me. I crashed.

Grief never asked permission to visit me. It just barged in like the suffocating wind of a tornado's vortex. It threw off a heavy shroud of longing for Werner and hung it on me. Grief never visited alone. It came with its entourage. One called *inconsolable* embraced me. One called *irrational desire* led me into the room of irrational thought. Grief knew nothing about common sense. *If I see Werner one more time, I'll be okay. I'll look at his picture. His picture will console me.* I picked up his photograph and looked at it. His fixed smile and beautiful brown eyes stared back at me. I touched its flatness. He was now only a picture in the house. I slammed the picture face down on the table. It only increased my ache to hear his voice. I stretched out my hand to touch him somewhere in the beyond, but the beyond was out of my reach. Mocking my gesture, grief's entourage whispered those hated words, *He's gone, he's gone.* I sank back down into the chair and became unglued.

Somewhere in my mind a small voice said, *Fight back or this shroud of longing will suffocate you.* I grabbed a book from the table next to my chair and randomly opened it. I'll read. Reading will get my focus back. Two words on the top of the page read, "Everlasting Consolation." I stared at the words, wiped my tears and read on . . .

> *Consolation*—there is music in the word. Like David's harp, it charms away the evil spirit of melancholy. All earthborn consolations are fleeting in essence and short lived in their existence. They are brilliant and fragile as the rainbow hues of a soap bubble, but the consolation that God gives does not fade nor lose its freshness. It stands all tests, the shock of trial, the passing years, and death itself.

The next sentence held the weapon that loosened grief's grip on me: "Are you pining and refusing to be comforted? Is this honorable to God? Cheer up. Jesus gives eternal consolation." (C. H. Spurgeon, *Evening by Evening*.)

Perhaps, I said to the question. *Perhaps consolation is not what I want. Perhaps I want the prize I had, my husband.* As quickly as I responded to the question, the defense I often used against grief's onslaught came to mind. *If you allow even the impossibility of that thought to take a breath in your mind, Werner would suffer again, you would have to say good-bye to him again.* No, I never want him back here to make my life bearable. I slowly calmed down.

When I went to bed later that night, sleep eluded me. Emotionally exhausted from another walk in the fire of sorrow, I gave up the bed and knelt at my open window. The blackness magnified the stars' brilliance. As I knelt under the millions of stars looking down at me, I thought of the other sleepless nights that sent me out of my bed and to the window for a midnight rendezvous with God.

One of those recurring dreams woke me up. In the dream Werner stood near me, yet distant and silent. The other woman was there. She always was there. The woman I came to understand represented death. Werner was powerless to escape her beckoning. She always took him from me. The dream always woke me.

I climbed out from under the down covers of the antique sleigh bed, went to the tall heavy double windows, and pushed them wide open. The cool February night breeze brushed past me. The boxwood hedges and poplar trees surrounding the chateau stood like silhouetted sentinels against the sky. Magnificent infinite indigo touched the rolling hills of the French countryside's horizon.

The night sky became my sanctuary and the windowsill my altar. It brought me closer to heaven's door, where I had an interest. I always imagined God standing in the doorway, and beside Him stood Werner, perfect and healed.

Sophistication is not a needy child's requirement. "God," I said, "I just need to know You are here. Send a shooting star so that I know You hear me." I felt silly to make such a childish request. Moments later, my eyes grew big like a child who received an unexpected gift.

A star shot out across the dark sky, followed right behind by another star. Down they fell together and disappeared into the night. I guess I forgot I was a child of God. He didn't. He breathed His consolation across the heavens and blew two stars out of place to reassure me of His presence.

In April I left France and traveled to Switzerland where I spent a few weeks with Werner's family, who were very special to me. However, I had a love-hate relationship with being in Switzerland. Everything Swiss spoke of Werner. Everywhere I went the presence of his absence accompanied me as a constant reminder of the remnant of our marriage.

One night, before I traveled up into the Alps to the village where Werner was born and where we were married, a flood of memories sent sleep flying from me and sent me fleeing to my bedroom window, where I sought God's protection against grief's imminent attack.

I opened the long windows above my bed, but the night wind rushed into the room too cold for me to rest my elbows on the windowsill. I left the windows wide open, and I slipped back under the down quilt. Under the night sky that became my canopy, I wrestled with the painful and difficult challenges tomorrow's journey presented. I asked God to let me go forward under His arms of support and courage.

I must walk to the churchyard where thirty-three years ago the laughter of family and friends filled the air, and all the church bells joyously rang out across the valley to celebrate our wedding day. A few months ago I walked with my family to that same churchyard. We walked to the cemetery under the awful toll of a lone bell's drone across the valley.

Tomorrow I cannot take that walk to Werner's grave for the first time since his burial in my own strength. Help me tonight to get through this unbearable anticipation by sending a . . . I stopped.

He is not your magician, I reminded myself. However, my distress wasn't insignificant to God. His ways are not dependent on my temporal view of Him.

There it came—a brilliant lone star fell down the night sky, sent, in perfect time, to prepare me to walk on in His strength. Once again He spread His rod and staff across the heavens to comfort me.

As I knelt at my bedroom window, after this long August day of wedding work, I realized during the past year I had traveled many miles physically, emotionally,

and spiritually. I recalled the times despair pushed me to
the end of my coping skills, God reached down and
scooped me up in His everlasting arms of comfort. In the
midst of my darkest nights, He set the stars in motion to
light my path. The warm August air settled quietly on
my flesh. God's breath of peace settled softly around my
spirit.

*In a few weeks I face a new transition. Life will begin
over again in a new home. I know You will prepare the
way.* I spoke to Him up to where a few stars struggled to
shine out from the darkest place in the sky.

All of a sudden a brilliant triangular banner of sizzling yellows burst out of that darkness and flew across
space like a mini firework. *Wow!* I said. Was my meteor
display a coincidence? Who cares? God cared enough to
place me at the window in His perfect time.

I knelt by the window a while longer. Awe and hum-
ble gratitude kept me there. *Not once, not twice, but three
times,* I thought, *the God of the universe sent down His
heavenly night messengers to lift me out of the valley of
grief's grip.* The stars, like the soap bubbles, were short-
lived. However, unlike the soap bubbles blown up by
human breath, God made the shooting stars. The words
"everlasting consolation" swept through me like a lul-
laby's soothing melody. I went to bed and slept.

CHAPTER 5

Dreaming of Tomorrow

Don't worry about tomorrow, because tomorrow will have its own worries. Each day has enough trouble of its own.
(Matthew 6:34)

The old hymn says, "Tomorrow will be better, wait and see." And we like to believe that, don't we? Especially when life is not going as smoothly as we like, we just want to get *through* today and on to tomorrow when surely things will improve. The Bible says repeatedly, "This, too, shall *pass*." And we hang on to that promise fiercely, because if the tough times we're suffering have come to *stay*, we surely can't take it. We want to run away. Escape. Leave today behind. So we are constantly dreaming of tomorrow and the promise of a better day.

Just Say Yes

BARBARA HOUGHTELING

E ntrepreneurs run in my family. My grandparents
went from farming to owning small businesses and
then a factory that produced baby booties. Dad built his
own law practice from the ground up. Mom founded a
natural foods store in Denver. As a teenager, I worked
behind the counter. I watched Mom turn her business
into a success and decided that as soon as I could, I'd
start my own business too. My family showed me what
it took: hard work, patience, faith, determination.

"You have to crawl before you can walk," my mother
warned me, "and walk before you can run."

As it turned out, I would need all the help I could get,
and then some.

My start in business was definitely at a crawl. One of
my first products was a health drink a friend had developed called New Moon tea. I spent months trying to sell
it to restaurants and supermarkets, but I could never get
it to catch on. Next I opened a used-clothing store in
Denver. That didn't feel right either. I knew that if I just
had the right product, I could put all my energy and faith

into making it a success. And the right product was out there, I was sure of it.

I worked part-time at a boutique on Sundays, hoping that would give me a better sense of what people were buying. The shop sold clothes and accessories for kids. I noticed that the items for babies sold best of all. What about baby booties? My grandparents had made them. They were relatively inexpensive and easy to produce, and they sold well. But mine had to be different, special somehow.

One morning I woke up before dawn with the design for a new kind of baby bootie imprinted on my mind. It was the oddest thing. So I slipped out of bed and went right to my sewing table. I had some quilted fabric lying around; the material was soft and easy to manipulate. I made a pattern, cut it out, and began to sew.

Most booties looked like socks, but I made mine wrap around the ankle so they'd be easier to slip onto a wiggly baby's foot. I pressed snaps into the fabric so the booties would stay on securely.

I tried them out on my neighbor's baby, Dustin. He scooted happily across the living-room carpet.

"You can't have them back," my neighbor joked. "Not unless you make me another pair."

I was on to something!

I did my homework. I experimented with different types of fabric, talked to suppliers, and worked out the costs of producing booties. If I was going to do this, I wanted to do it right.

I named my booties "Scootees." I made the first batch at home, sitting at my kitchen table. I cut the fabric and sewed, and my husband, Gary, a builder, used his strong hands to press on the snaps. I drove down to Denver with my Scootees on the seat beside me and shopped them around to different kids stores. Orders started coming, a couple dozen pairs at first, then a couple hundred.

We rented a building in nearby Tabernash as a base for the company—which we called Alpine Ventures—and bought used sewing machines and an enormous clicker press to cut the fabric. We also hired a sales representative. One day near the end of May he called me.

"Are you sitting down?" he asked. "I showed your Scootees to Kids R Us. They love them. They want to put them in their stores in three months. Can you do that?"

"Definitely," I said, trying to contain my excitement. "How many do they want?"

"Seventeen thousand pairs."

I almost dropped the receiver. Only in my dreams had I ever thought we would get an order that large. This is the opportunity of a lifetime, I reminded myself. Just say yes!

"Yes!"

I got a credit line from the bank, using our house as collateral. Gary had just finished a building job, so he came to help me full time. We worked eighteen hours a day, making, wrapping, and packaging booties. We rationed our sleep from six hours to five, then to four, catching naps on the couch in the office whenever we had a spare minute. We hired more people, stopping folks in the street and putting them to work packing booties. We loaded the truck a half hour before the deadline, but we made it. As soon as Kids R Us got the shipment, they put in another order, this time for another 13,000 pairs to be in their stores by Christmas.

Just say yes, I reminded myself.

"It's a deal," I told our rep. This time, I was confident. We'd proved to ourselves that we could fill one big order. We could do another. No problem.

We bought a new building, this time in Granby, another little mountain town, and went straight to work. By Gary's birthday a week later, we had the first part of the shipment—4,000 pairs of booties—done. As I locked up the building that night, I looked over all the packed boxes, ready to go. An immense feeling of relief swept over me. We had made it. We had a steady client. All that hard work had paid off, and the business was finally taking off. I could relax.

The phone woke me up that night. The clock read midnight.

"This is the Granby fire department. I think you'd better come quick."

We sped the few miles to Granby. A dim orange glow lit the night sky.

"The business!"

Granby's volunteer fire department was already there. Flames licked up through the shattered windows and the holes in the roof. All the planning. All the hard work. All our hopes. What could I do but cry as I watched everything go up in smoke?

Gary and I drove home sometime after dawn, staring at the road and trying to console each other. We had taken such a huge leap of faith. Now everything we'd built up, all of our hard work and success, had vanished in a single night.

Gary went straight to bed. I called my dad. I told him about the fire, the booties that had been ready to ship, the order for Kids R Us that we still had to fill. He was silent for a moment.

"You've shown me that you can build a business," he said. "Now show me that you can rebuild one."

With what? I wondered. Everything is gone. Still, something urged me to go back to our factory. I let Gary sleep and got in the car. At the building, I walked through the ruins. Scorched and soggy booties were scattered in the basement. The shipment was unsalvageable. So were all our records. But I saw that most of the damage on the sewing machines was just from soot and steam. And the expensive clicker press—our most important machine—

was untouched. Was it a sign? Don't give up. Just say yes.

The mayor of Granby came to see me.

"A number of local businesses have already offered to help you," he said, handing me a list of vacant commercial spaces for rent. I felt like crying again. This time for joy. We had the tools. We had the space. All we needed was money.

Later that day I talked with the insurance company. They had determined that the fire started with a crack in the chimney lining that their inspector had missed. We would be covered for the damage to the business and for the full market value of the lost booties.

We used the insurance money to install a computer system to replace our old files. I called Kids R Us and made a compromise. We'd get them the most popular colors and sizes in time for Christmas, then fill the rest of the shipment as soon as possible. We impressed them with our effort and won a customer for life.

Scootees became one of the top-selling baby booties in the country. I have stopped making them now, but they're still on the market, and I've developed lots more products for babies, from bibs to crib sheets. Gary and I have even made some babies of our own—three, in fact. My business success didn't start with the idea for Scootees. It didn't even start when we completed that first big order. I believe it started with the fire—or the day after. That was when I learned to say yes when the answer looks like no. It takes a lot of things to be an entrepreneur. But faith, faith in yourself and your ideas, faith that you will be rewarded for your efforts, is the most important of all.

Bill's Strength

CHERYL ABBOTT

To a lot of people, the empty nest syndrome may mean loneliness or the end of something good and happy. But to Bill and me? We were looking forward to being empty nesters and about all the plans we were making. Our youngest son was a senior in high school, and, to tell the truth, our approaching empty nest was looking pretty good to us. We were beginning to plan weekend getaways and exciting vacations.

What we hadn't planned was Bill becoming sick. At first, he was told that his problems were due to work-related stress. Bill became increasingly ill, and our concerns grew as he continued getting worse. After more tests were done, we finally received the diagnosis that we hadn't expected—the "C" word. Bill had stage four colon cancer.

After the initial shock, we were numb, barely able to believe what we now knew to be true; but as we cycled through all the emotions that come with such devastating news, we slowly formulated a simple plan: we wanted to "keep life normal." We had all the tools we needed to fight a long, hard battle against cancer. We had a large and loving family, dependable friends, caring church family, supportive employers and coworkers, and aggressive doctors. But most important, we had our loving God who had promised to provide for all our needs. With that decision made, the fight against cancer began. I never realized at the time what a difficult struggle "keeping life normal" was going to be.

As sick as Bill became during his treatments, he was the most amazing man I have ever known. He faced the battle of his life with endless strength, courage, and an incredible attitude. He knew well that the odds were against him, but he was determined to do everything he could to beat cancer and enjoy a long life, looking forward to seeing his grandchildren grow up.

When chemotherapy treatments made Bill so sick that he lost his hair and could not find the strength to get out of bed, he was optimistic about it and felt that being sick was a very good sign that the chemo was working.

As the one-year anniversary of his diagnosis approached, Bill surprised me by saying, "Let's go celebrate!" He felt that after one year of treatment, we had a lot to celebrate, and he was right. We really did have reason to celebrate God's blessing of allowing Bill to come so far with his treatments and the support and love provided by our family, friends, church, and community. One by one we remembered and cherished each blessing God has so richly poured over us.

Even though he was so sick, Bill continued to work,

most of the time driving one hundred and ten miles a day to work. He had clients who needed help, and they were very patient with his erratic hours, most never realizing how sick he really was, because Bill was determined to "keep life normal."

Then the day came, two and a half years after Bill's diagnosis, when we received the news that no other treatment options were available and that the doctors would try to keep Bill "as comfortable as possible." This news was probably the hardest we had heard since being told that he had cancer, and I felt as though I had been knocked flat.

As we were driving home with the finality of this diagnosis, Bill said, in his quiet way, "When you tell everyone, don't make this bigger than it is." I was already struggling to keep from bursting into tears in front of him, tears of both grief and anger that I was losing my husband and best friend. Bill's requesting that I "don't make this bigger than it is" went very deep. My first thought was *Hello—you're dying—soon, and that's not a big deal?* When I told him how I felt about his request, his quiet comeback was, "The big deal was being told I had cancer; this is just the natural progression." Such wisdom, such "grace under fire"—yet this was always his way.

Have you ever asked yourself the question, "If you knew you were dying tomorrow, how would you spend your last day?" For us, we lived the answer to that question seven more months, keeping in mind Bill's request to "keep life as normal as possible." We lived every day to the fullest.

Bill enjoyed each day and rarely complained, even when I knew his pain level was almost beyond his endurance. During the time Bill was taking radiation treatments at the cancer center, he also worked, spent time with family and friends, and we went to the lake as often as possible. He would walk through the house and remind me that "next spring you need to . . ." which was clearly his way of gently preparing me for his absence. We read books to prepare us for the end of life, discussing his preferences on how to handle his passing and his memorial service.

Bill continued to work until two weeks prior to his death. He even bought thank-you gifts for several of his closest friends and took time to tell each of his children how proud he was of them and their accomplishments. There was always a lot of laughter in our house—but we had good-natured laughter, many times at his expense, because of the funny things he might say or do because of the medications he was taking.

In the final days of Bill's life, he greeted family and friends and accepted their loving good-byes, and on an icy night in Feburary, God honored our prayers for Bill to pass to heaven with just the two of us there—"no big deal."

I'm quite certain there was a big deal in heaven that night.

The Stolen Car

DONNA COLLINS TINSLEY

I don't need a caretaker and don't try to take care of me!" No, Mama didn't come right out and say that but it was obvious that was how she felt. Stubborn? She always accused me of that trait, but I guess it was transferred genetically. But I couldn't persuade her.

At age sixty-two my mom was still a feisty woman. She went on, doggedly caring for her bedridden husband and her little great-granddaughter, Aubrey, the light of her life.

Mama had worked hard in her younger days to put food on the table for four children because her second husband was in prison. She survived that "marriage from hell" to marry again, happily, to Poppa. For the first time she, along with Poppa, owned a home.

When they had bought the house over thirty years ago, the neighborhood was decent and quiet. Poppa had taken such pride in adding on and fixing it up. When the small house next door came up for sale, he was quick to buy it for his "retirement" income. But the neighborhood in the ensuing years became more run down. People were leaving the area, and renters weren't taking care of the homes. Kids, hanging out and bored with nothing of worth to do, often ended up getting into trouble. Nearly all the little girls in the neighborhood seemed to grow up too fast: the next thing you knew they were unwed mothers.

Retirement came early to Poppa, as he had been exposed to asbestos on his jobs as an electrician. He and Mama would end up needing help at fairly young ages when Mama's diabetes worsened. She finally agreed to hire a young couple to help her out, and they lived in the little house next door.

The only time I could get Mama to let me take care of her was after she had diabetes-related surgery on her foot. Aubrey stayed at her brother's house, and the care-takers stayed with Poppa. When she left the hospital, she came home with my family for a short time. Never one to be idle, she was anxious to get home. Even spending extra time with my daughters (then ages five, eight, and eleven) as they camped out with her in our family room did not deter her from her goal.

"They need me, Donna," she said. "When Aubrey comes back home, I know life will be back to normal!" She left our home as soon as the doctor said she could, happy to be taking care of Poppa and Aubrey again.

One morning a few months later, Mama phoned me saying frantically, "Donna, someone stole my car last night!"

"How could that have happened, Mama?" I said. "You and Poppa installed that light to activate when someone comes around, and the caretakers are in the little house right next door! Have you called the police?" I questioned.

"Yes, they filed a report. And Donna, my purse was in the trunk! I was carrying in groceries and somehow my purse fell in when I got the groceries out. I just forgot about it until now," she said. "I'm going to have to go and get a new driver's license and everything!"

"I'll be there as soon as I can," I promised. During the drive I imagined what had happened. Although the caretakers stayed on after she returned home, I often found when I visited her that Mama was still cooking and cleaning for everyone. Poor in the riches of this world, she was rich in love and generosity, and the whole neighborhood knew where to come if they were hungry. And between caring for Poppa and Aubrey, Mama often got busy and left things in the car. We always laughed and called it her senior moments.

Poor thing, she was having a hard time feeling at peace, and who could blame her? I didn't tell Mama what I was thinking: *if the car could be stolen so easily, what might happen next?*

"Mama, why don't you and Poppa sell both houses and come live near me?" It wasn't the first time I had suggested this. Even though I knew Mama wanted to be independent. I was always looking near my home for something that might be affordable.

"No, Donna, I love this house and living in Holly Hill. All my friends are here! I'll get my helper to take me to get a new driver's license, but please pray that we will find the car."

"Okay, Mama, I'll pray and also call the Prayer Line on the radio." Later, when I called the noon prayer requests, they prayed for the return of the car and her purse, intact.

Mama wanted everyone to know what had happened, so she called my sister, Jeannine, who lives in Louisiana. So when I went home, I called my brothers to let them know. My brother, Charles, who is a laid-back sort of guy, wasn't too worried.

"Don't worry, sis, I'll get by and check on them," he said.

However, my other brother, Dale, who lived in North Carolina, decided to drive down with a van that his family wasn't using so Mama wouldn't have to depend on the caretakers for transportation. I had been hoping Dale would come and visit Mama, as he wasn't able to when she was hospitalized for high blood pressure, congestive heart failure, or the diabetes surgery in November. His family wasn't able to come for Christmas either, and I had been feeling that he needed to visit. So his visit would be a double blessing.

Mama was so excited about Dale coming down it nearly made her forget about her troubles. His oldest daughter, Jessica, was coming down with him. Miraculously, shortly before Dale arrived, the car was found at a little strip mall. Not only was it intact, but her purse was there with nothing missing!

Lord, why did this happen? I wondered. It seemed so strange: the car stolen and then found. Did Dale waste his time in bringing the van? Yet I knew enough about the Lord to know He works all things for our good, even the seemingly illogical ones.

Since it had been a stressful week, I went and got little Aubrey for the weekend. That left more time for Dale and Jessica to visit uninterrupted with Mama and Poppa. After being away so long, I knew they had a lot of catching up to do.

Unexpectedly, Monday morning our precious mother passed away! A sudden heart attack and she passed away at home before the paramedics could get there. Amidst the pain and grief, I realized if the car hadn't been stolen there was no chance she would have seen her younger son and granddaughter before she died. Coincidence? I don't think so.

"And we know that all that happens to us is working for our good if we love God and are fitting into his plans" (Romans 8:28 TLB).

The Lord used a stolen car to bring about the unspoken hope of a mother's heart: to see her son one last time. He will use whatever it takes in our lives to bring about His will for our good.

Even a stolen car.

All She Had Was Faith and Five Dollars

KENNETH HEACOCK

My daughter hadn't said much all afternoon during her weekly visit. I couldn't even get her to smile, which was unusual. "Honey, I can sense there's something wrong. Anything you want to talk about?

She sighed and shook her head, but I can be persuasive. She finally broke down and said, "Dad, our financial problems are overwhelming me. We've been working so hard, but we only seem to get deeper in the hole. And we don't want a handout. I'm so worried, I can't even think straight."

I knew just what to say. Patting her hand, I nodded and said, "Let me tell you a story about your great-grandmother.

"As you know, I grew up on a dairy farm just outside a tiny town called Sac City, Iowa. When I was a little boy, my grandmother lived with us for a while. She was a very religious woman. Many of her ancestors had been

German ministers, and she shared their strong faith and belief in God, hard work, and giving to the Lord.

We didn't have nursing homes in those days. Or Social Security. Family took care of family. Having borne thirteen children, my grandma had plenty of homes to visit. I loved it when she stayed with us on our farm.

Our large wooden frame farmhouse boasted a rambling front porch. On warm Iowa summer evenings, Grandma sat in her rocking chair on that porch after having helped with chores indoors, in spite of her aging rheumatism. When finished with morning chores, she would rock in her chair for a while and observe the activities of the farm. Our porch gave a good view of our land that sprawled across acres of flat Iowa terrain. The harnesses of our two teams of horses jingled as Dad readied Bob, Prince, Ted, and Daisy for the day's work.

No, we didn't have gasoline tractors back then. Your grandpa used steam-driven tractors to operate the threshing machines. After the wheat or barley was threshed, separating the grain from the stems, the stems were stacked and used as bedding for the animals. Nothing was wasted. Your two aunts and uncle and I had a great time sliding down the sides of those haystacks.

On cold Iowa winter nights, the fireplace in our living room invited our family to be together. Grandma loved to sit in front of that fireplace, reading her Bible every night. I remember curling up beside the rhythmic creaking of that rocking chair and listening as she read aloud Bible stories, making them come to life. She read the Bible in its entirety several times throughout her lifetime.

"God will take care of you if you do your part first, no questions asked," she would say.

She'd sit with her high-top button shoes, floor-length comfortable dresses, and ever-present apron, smoking her corncob pipe. I remember the sweet smell of tobacco filling the room, mingling with the aroma of the logs burning in the fire, the smoke curling around her head. We knew she was finished enjoying her smoke for the day when we heard the whack, whack, whack of that corncob pipe on the arm of her rocker, knocking the ashes into the ash bowl below.

In 1932 I graduated from high school. The Depression was at its darkest stages and we lost our farm. Many people throughout the country had no food to eat. Food lines were everywhere. Businesses and homes were lost. People couldn't get jobs. It was a frightening time.

I had been dreaming of going to college for some time but knew we couldn't afford it, so I forced myself to accept the situation and looked for a job doing anything I could to help the family. My disappointment crushed me.

At this time a recruiter from a private college called Carleton, 230 miles away in Minnesota, came to Sac City looking for potential students. I had been a good student in high school, especially math and science, and I was an athlete. The recruiter was impressed with me and said he'd get back to me.

I remember staring in disbelief at the letter informing me of the scholarship. I could barely breathe, afraid that if I took a deep breath I would wake up and discover it was all just a dream. College! The possibility of a bright future was within my grasp after all.

Then reality set in. I had no money for transportation. How would I even get there? And if I could get there, how would I eat? There were no jobs in Sac City and no way to earn any money for the necessities. My dream vanished. There was no use even thinking about it. It just wasn't possible. The letdown threatened to overwhelm me as I stared out the window, crumpling the letter in my hand.

It was then that my grandmother burst into action. After watching me mope around the house for days, she sat me down and said, "Kenneth, you have to stop thinking so negatively. It's not what you don't have. It's what you do have. And what you do have is a scholarship, the ability to work hard, and a God that will provide the rest. Quit worrying about the rest. It'll come. Just go to college and work hard. Everything else will fall into place."

Then she took her wrinkled hands, hands that had labored for eighty-three years, hands that had cradled thirteen children, and dug into the folds of her long skirt, withdrawing from her deep pocket a five-dollar bill. She tucked the bill into my shirt pocket.

"You take this five dollars. It's all I have. But with this and faith in the Almighty, all your needs will be provided. I'm sure of it." She smiled and hugged me. Not only did she have faith in God, but she also had faith in my abilities.

So with nothing but the clothes on my back, butterflies in my stomach, and a five-dollar bill in my pocket, I set out on the road to my future. My childhood home I had always loved stretched out behind me as I hitchhiked east on Highway 20 and then north on Interstate 35, totaling 230 miles to Northfield, Minnesota.

Throughout those four years at Carleton College, I worked as a dishwasher in a restaurant, and that's where I met the owner's daughter—your mother. I graduated in 1936 after studying zoology and chemistry and have been teaching high school ever since. We haven't been financially rich, but we've always been able to pay our bills and put food on the table for you six kids. God has been faithful.

Grandma died in 1939 at the age of ninety. Her faith never wavered, even during the Depression. She didn't need money to know the Great Provider will meet our needs even during difficult times, as long as we fulfill our tasks and keep moving forward. Faith in God and five dollars was all she ever needed."

My daughter hugged me, and a smile began to spread across her face. "Thanks, Dad. I knew you'd have the answer."

More Than Football

MIKE HOLMGREN

From the time I was old enough to pass a football, I dreamed of playing professionally. I grew up in an apartment above my grandparents' bakery in the shadow of Kezar Stadium, then home of the San Francisco 49ers. My PB&Js were never made on Wonder Bread, and I was very aware of the NFL. I was also aware that God had given me above-average athletic ability.

While some of my friends struggled to make the varsity football team at Lincoln High School, it came pretty easy to me. I was the starting quarterback my junior and senior years and received a full scholarship to the University of Southern California.

I could hardly contain my excitement the summer before I left for Los Angeles to begin my freshman year. My plans to play pro football were on track. Unfortunately, my walk with the Lord wasn't. It had almost come to a standstill.

Every Sunday I had attended church with my extended family. And during sixth grade I became a follower of Jesus after listening to Billy Graham preach at the Cow Palace auditorium. Graham's words made sense to me, and I realized I needed to have a personal relationship with Christ.

But the success I'd experienced as a high school athlete had taken its toll. I was more Mike-conscious than God-conscious. I soon discovered that the Lord has a way of bringing back those who belong to him.

Shortly after joining the USC Trojans, I suffered an injury in practice that would keep me sidelined for most of my college career. For the first time in life, things weren't falling into place. My ego was bruised and my hopes dashed.

My coaches and the scouts who saw me play, however, were sufficiently impressed with my talent and potential. I was drafted by the St. Louis Cardinals by the time I graduated in 1970 with a degree in English and education. My dreams of playing in the NFL would finally be fulfilled.

But my days with St. Louis were numbered. I was cut during the preseason. A couple weeks later I was picked up by the New York Jets. I was excited. The Jets were a powerhouse under the quarterbacking genius of "Broadway Joe" Namath. With the start of the season less than a month away, I was confident I had landed a place on the team.

Then the unexpected happened. A veteran quarterback from another team became available, and the Jets signed him as a backup to Namath. I was sent packing, blindsided and brokenhearted.

To be honest, I was crushed. My only goal in life had been to play professional football, and God had allowed that goal not to be realized. I hadn't been giving God much attention during those days. Now I was angry at Him.

The five-hour flight from New York back home to San Francisco seemed twice as long. I remember my dad picking me up at the airport and attempting to console me. I felt like a total failure. I knew Dad had been extremely proud of me. Now having been drafted and cut twice, I felt like I had let him down.

My sense of failure eventually pointed me in God's direction. In the following months I picked up my Bible for the first time in a long time. Proverbs 3:5-6 stood out like a neon sign: "Trust in the LORD with all your heart and lean not on your own understanding; in all your ways acknowledge him, and he will make your paths straight."

I couldn't understand why my lifelong dream was dashed, but I determined to trust the Lord and recommit my life to Him.

A girl whom I had met at junior high summer camp re-entered my life. Kathy had just graduated from a Christian college and was working as a short-term missionary in Africa. Her letters encouraged me in my spiritual growth.

Within a year Kathy and I were married. I also landed a job teaching drafting and coaching football and tennis at Sacred Heart High School in San Francisco. Kathy and I had twin daughters, and life was full and good. My thoughts of the NFL had been buried for good.

After ten years at the high school level, I was given a chance to coach at San Francisco State University. Kathy and I had two more daughters. My career consisted of coaching all men, yet at the end of the day I found myself the only male in a house full of women. It was amazing.

From San Francisco we moved to Brigham Young University, where I accepted an assistant coaching job. Because of my growing faith, I struggled with the decision of being employed by a Mormon school. But in keeping with Proverbs 3:5-6, I sensed the Lord directing our paths. He made it clear we could let our lights shine and make a difference.

We had some impressive seasons at BYU, and the head coach of the San Francisco 49ers sought me out. Bill Walsh asked if I would consider joining his staff as quarterback coach. I couldn't believe it. After nearly fifteen years my dream of an NFL career was back on track. Not as a player, but as a coach. We could see the Lord's fingerprints all over the place.

From 1984 to 1991 I had the privilege of working with Joe Montana and an extremely gifted group of players.

Coach Walsh was a brilliant teacher and mentor. Like the original 49er miners, the namesake of San Francisco's football team, we struck gold big-time. We won two Super Bowl rings during the years I was with the team.

The last couple years I was with the 49ers, I had offers from NFL teams to become a head coach. I was really tempted, but as I looked at the needs of my wife and daughters I knew the timing was bad. Moving the twins during high school wouldn't have been fair to them.

The media criticized my decisions. Columnists essentially wrote that I would never again be given the chance to become a head coach. My colleagues said much the same thing. As in other times of confusion, I committed my way to the Lord.

God proved my critics wrong. Two years later, the Green Bay Packers invited me to become their head coach. Talk about a dream come true. I was following in the footsteps of the legendary Vince Lombardi. By the time I left the Packers in 1998, we had made back-to-back Super Bowl appearances and in 1997 won the Packers' first Super Bowl championship since Super Bowl II in 1968.

Leaving Green Bay while the momentum was building was hard. Life had become comfortable, and being a winning coach in that small Wisconsin city was the equivalent to being governor of the state. I even had a street named after me. But I was offered an amazing opportunity to try to build a football dynasty in Seattle. I couldn't refuse.

The first years in Seattle were anything but easy. I had gone from back-to-back Super Bowls to struggling to get the Seahawks into postseason play. And then my personal world collapsed. Kathy was diagnosed with breast cancer. I was devastated. Everything I'd accomplished professionally had been with her at my side. I couldn't imagine life without her. The thought of possibly losing my life partner and best friend made my hopes for building a championship team seem insignificant. Once again I turned to the Lord and claimed the promises in the third chapter of Proverbs.

Our family pulled together as never before during Kathy's illness. Thankfully, God answered our prayers. The doctors' treatments were effective. The cancer disappeared. In the midst of the stress of health issues and challenges with team personnel and injuries, I was tempted to resign my position before the 2005 season. But Kathy encouraged me to hang in there.

I'm so glad I did. I never imagined that 2005 would be the storybook season it turned out to be: twelve consecutive victories, the Seahawks' first playoff victory in twenty-three years, an NFC Championship and a bid to play in Super Bowl XL.

Although the outcome against the Pittsburgh Steelers was not what we had hoped for, I was extremely proud of our team. They had every reason to hold their heads high.

Following that Super Bowl, the Seahawks offered me a two-year extension on my contract. It might have seemed like an easy decision. But it wasn't. I wanted to make sure my family was OK with it. I also needed to check in with my heavenly Father. After all, He's been the one who has coached me for the past four decades.

After much prayer and reflection (and a few days chilling on the hot sands of Maui), I felt God encouraging me to go for it. Even though the defeats and challenges continue in addition to the wins and opportunities, I know I can trust the Lord for what lies ahead. I have learned from personal experience that my heavenly Coach is in control.

The Music Still Plays

REBECCA BARLOW JORDAN

I first heard the music as a child when my mother's slender fingers danced across the ivories. She and others patiently taught me how to play as well. But when college called, then marriage, I left my piano behind. Could I still hear the music?

Soon after that, as a young mother in my twenties, I remember standing at the kitchen window one day asking God to fill my heart with a song that would not end. A melody that would linger long after the notes had hushed. Not a masterpiece, not a classic, but a simple melody that would continue through all of the major and minor notes of life. A song that could put a smile on the heart even when all known instruments of joy were silent.

Months later, we discovered the beauties of Colorado as a family. The Rocky Mountain grandeur, the cool mountain streams, and early morning sunrises took my breath away and literally made me break out in sponta- neous melody: "The hills are alive with the sound of music!" And they were. I found that out one morning as we stayed with our friends at their Colorado cabin.

Many summers, in the early mornings, I would steal away to the river just below their cabin. With the orange sun peeking over the blue horizon, and a chorus of aspens whistling in rhythm to the rippling waters, I would sit spellbound and just listen. No keyboard could capture this melody, for it was the music of the soul.

As I pored over the pages of familiar Scriptures, it was as if notes began to dance on the page by an invisible hand. I had never had such a feeling of awe, of amazement, of gratitude. A divine, inaudible voice seemed to whisper through God's creations: "Come—and the music will begin." Each time I would come, thirsty, eager to drink of God's life-giving water, and anxious to hear the promised melodies.

And then I heard them. *Of course,* I thought. *How simple.* Weaving together some basic notes from my childhood storehouse, I began to sing the songs He gave me. Most of the words were not original with me. His words—Scripture—sung back to Him in new melodies. What a wonderful way to remember His own letters to me!

In the months and years that followed, while the children attended school, I found myself lingering more and more in the mornings at our makeshift desk back home. But this time, with pen in hand, I wrote furiously, recording new words, pictures of joy in the morning, cries for hope in the darkness, melodies that freed my spirit—just like my experiences on those crisp, cool,

Colorado mornings. On some days, an inner voice chided me, "Why are you wasting so much time?" Then I'd look at the clock, think of the fresh mound of chores and laundry waiting, and pack away my songs.

That's when I remembered again that sinful woman's gift—the expensive vial of perfume poured out on the feet of Jesus. Wasteful? Perhaps. But not to Jesus. You see, each one of us has a song in our hearts just waiting for a recital. It doesn't matter if anyone ever hears it or not. Some songs are given just for the ears of you and your Lover. Like Solomon and his bride, we abandon ourselves to the very One who can make the music sweet—the One who writes the melody for us— so that we can sing it back to Him.

My own children learned to play their simple melodies, and make beautiful music as blithe fingers glided over those ivory piano keys. And I played too, occasionally—for church, for myself—and yes, for the Lover of my soul. Sometimes I sang my songs to others; many more lie inside a folder in my file cabinet. A waste of time? I think not. I still sing His songs regularly, in church, at home, wherever I go. It dances in my smile— and sometimes in my fingers when I sign a song to Him in sign language. I have learned that you cannot escape the magnetism of the mysterious melody in our spirits. Once awakened, beauty will not be silent. Never.

God answered my wistful prayer years ago as I stood

by that kitchen window. Years later in the blackness of my soul, when depression stalked unmercifully; when another tried to steal the shreds of my dignity; when illness knocked repeatedly; when prayers went unanswered or on hold; when death carried away part of my heart—even through it all, the song He gave me has never died. He stirred up that melody I had heard as a young child. He heard the yearnings of a young mother eager to please. And God has kept His song alive.

As I look back over the years, I've been amazed at God's discernment, at how quickly He cuts through the heart of a problem and bares the interior of the soul. A few words carefully placed, like a surgeon's sharp instrument, and my defenses bleed away.

Could I still hear the music now? Recorded praise music fills my home daily—always at mealtime, and several times throughout the day. Of course I could hear the music. It was woof and warp, the fiber of my being.

But could I *really* still hear the music? I had to find out.

So I returned to the place where I first heard the mysterious melodies over twenty-five years ago. Eight years had passed since we had basked in the cool mountain air of Colorado. And for almost eight years, maybe more, the ivory keys in my home remained mostly silent.

After a brief stay in Colorado Springs, my husband and I headed toward Southwestern Colorado in our rented car. The pines grew taller and the mountains grew larger, it seemed, with every mile. Ever since our first visit to this magnificent vacation state, I had made the same statement: "When we cross the state line into Colorado, something in me just comes alive, and my spirit is set free." Each time I felt like laughing, playing, crying, praying, shouting, and dancing before the Lord— all at the same time.

But now I grew quieter as I listened. Like an orchestra leader, I tapped my finger on the window as if to call nature's instruments to attention. The music was about to begin. I could feel it in my spirit. Several hours later, we drove up to the homespun cabin of our friends.

I could hardly wait to rise early the next morning. With Bible, notebook, and pen in hand, I wrapped up in a sweater to face the morning chill and tiptoed out our friends' cabin door. On the front porch bench, with hot tea in hand, and a quilt snuggled about her shoulders, sat my girlfriend.

"Come, join me," she said. It had, after all, been years since we had shared a cup of fellowship together.

I sat for a moment, fidgeting. But I kept glancing toward the river. Sensing my uncertainty, she said, "It's okay if you want to be alone."

"Well, I uhm . . . sort of . . . wanted to go . . . down to the river," I stuttered.

I hated to abandon my hostess and friend, but I was

on a mission. So I headed toward the water. I spotted a large stone a few yards away, sat down, took a deep breath, opened my Bible, closed my eyes, and . . . listened. There they were—the familiar sounds of trickling water, the whistling of the aspens in the wind, and nature's winged chorus chirping their approval to this serene setting. I opened my eyes, and glanced down the river. A lone fisherman, casting his lure upon the water in rapid succession, waited expectantly for a trout to bite. Music to his ears.

And as I opened to the Psalms, I too, like the psalmist David, waited, casting my expectations before the Lord. How many times had David sat beside the still waters, listening to His Good Shepherd's voice, composing these melodies to the King. I thought of Jesus and how so much of His ministry took place around water: the calling of his fishermen disciples, the teaching and feeding of the multitudes, stilling the stormy Galilean waters. And often, the glassy sea became a bridge of refuge as He escaped from the press of the crowd and sought time with His beloved Father.

There it was again. That nagging question. *Could I still hear the music?* I chose a less familiar psalm and began to read silently.

And then like a whisper, a still small voice grew louder as the notes began to dance in my head. A phrase, then a few notes, a prayer, a hum. Soon a full-scale melody escaped my lips in quiet, hushed tones—so softly only the Lord and I could hear. But it was there. The music was there. Yes! It was short. But like the "Jesus People" of the '70s, whose bodies swayed and souls stirred with Scripture songs in our church youth groups, I simply took a single verse of Scripture and began humming a melody. God did the rest. My compositions would never top the charts, but hopefully they would tap the heart of God as I sang back the praises David so faithfully recorded so many years ago.

Reluctantly, we returned home several days later, leaving our friends and my beloved musical setting behind.

I've been thinking a lot lately about that closed keyboard in my living room. Life has a way of stilling the music at times, or of making us think we're too deaf to ever hear it again. If I could still hear the music in Colorado, why not here?

So not long ago I headed out to my backyard refuge. The only water sounds I heard there were the neighbor's sprinkler or the birds wallowing in my birdbath. My husband wanted to place a large boulder in the garden for my birthday to symbolize my beloved mountains, but the cost and carry was a little prohibitive for the time being. *Perhaps a fountain might help,* I thought, plotting next year's birthday wish.

As I settled into my hammock, the only whistling I

heard were the preschoolers' voices down the street, although on windy days, the trees in my backyard can compose a pretty decent melody.

I wonder. Can I still hear the music—here? I had lingered on my porch many times with Bible in hand. But how long had it been since I had heard a new melody? Was I playing the same old tune? Or worse still, had I silenced the music through neglect or slothfulness? So I took out my Bible and opened to Psalms. Once again, I closed my eyes, breathed a prayer, and asked God for the music to begin.

At first I heard nothing but nature's distractions—a fussy squirrel, a noisy bluejay, the sound of car horns in the distance. But as Jesus silenced my heart and stirred my longings, it was unmistakable. Only a few scattered notes at first. Then more. I looked up, drinking in with delight as heaven played its harmony with my crude efforts. That's when I discovered the secret. The one my Master Designer had been trying to tell me.

Perhaps you've been thinking throughout this story, *Oh brother! What a romantic you are! Get real. The music stopped in our household three weeks after we said, "I do." Peanut butter keeps all our ivory keys stuck together, and the house never gets quiet enough to hear my own voice over my teenager's CD—much less some "illusive" melody. I live in the real world, not in some writer's paradise. As far as vacations go? Mountains and rivers, and all that stuff? The mountainous piles of kids' laundry and the gurgling sounds of my washing machine draining are the closest I ever get to that. Of course there is some music—the kind I make when someone cuts me off on the freeway in 7:00 a.m. work traffic.*

Still another may say, *Of course you can still hear the music. You still have YOUR husband. You still have YOUR kids. Oh, I still hear the music, all right. But the melody sounds more like a funeral dirge for me.*

You're right, of course. Except for one thing. The secret. Music does not just whisper through the mountain forest or peaceful rivers. It will stream behind the raging rapids and burst through a splitting earthquake. Melodies are not locked inside romantic hideaways or tucked away in some tragic, forgotten corner. It does not take an orchestra to raise a heavenly symphony. It only takes one listener. Because, you see, music is in the ears of the beholder. And in the heart of the Lover.

Maybe it's time to move the pictures and dusty photographs and let the keys live again. The songs dance on the page and the computer in a different form now, but once in a while, I ache to give the ivories a chance to laugh and smile again—if only for Him, and maybe for me.

Waiting at the Window

PAULA HEMINGWAY

Growing up during those happy days of Hula-Hoops, hopscotch, and the hokey-pokey meant that much of my childhood I rocked around the clock playing those groovy games with my three sisters and the neighborhood kids.

Almost every day, though, my sisters and I would take a break from our girlish games to play another game that didn't involve rules or equipment but was infinitely more important. Late in the afternoon, we'd hop onto our old living room divan, lean against the back of the well-worn furniture, and peer through the front picture window to wait in excited anticipation for someone of more consequence to us than Shirley Temple, Elvis, or even the president of the United States. Our waiting was always rewarded when at last a bulky, dome-shaped white 1950s Buick my parents called "Ole Betsy" (they named everything) swung alongside the curb and stopped in front of our house. The car door slammed and out popped our hero.

All four of us dashed out of the house, jumping up

and down like pogo sticks yelling, "Daddy! Daddy!" Our long springy curls bounced as we raced down the sidewalk to hug and cling to his legs. He stiffly lumbered along the sidewalk saddled with the extra cargo of four little girls, but nevertheless relishing this daily homecoming routine after a demanding day. We cared little that Dad drove a clunker car or that we lived in a downscale house wearing nondesigner clothes. What counted was that Dad was there. We just loved our daddy.

I thank God that my daddy always came home. He never once stood us up. His commitment to Mom and us girls, solid as our saddle shoes, provided love, security, and protection for our family and a lifetime of trust in our heavenly Father.

As I grew into an adult, though, I had no inkling how that faith and trust in God would be tested. Somewhere along my life's journey, I bargained with God that if I live for Him, then nothing bad would happen to me or my family. Oh, I didn't make such a compact consciously, nor would I have admitted it out loud, but difficult events in my life drew out what was hiding behind the curtains. This window view, unlike my childhood home's picture window, was tinted by sorrow and pain that no window cleaner could wipe away.

Instead of leaning against the divan, now I'm sitting in the passenger seat peering out the window of my car at a beautiful spring day in Arkansas, the kind of day that calls for a picnic in the park or a stroll through the neighborhood. Such delightful diversions were not going to be a part of this day. Upon arrival at our parklike destination, I notice throngs of cars and people who are either clustered in groups or standing in a long line, waiting to greet our oldest daughter, Marla, and her husband, Nathan.

Although deeply touched by the presence of so many, my mind considers running away, but instead I get out of the car and traipse through the crowd, thanking friends and loved ones for coming. I take my seat under the tent and look straight ahead, noticing for the first time the tiny box in front of me. Caskets are supposed to be adult-lived-a-long-life size, not fifty-five-days-old-infant size. Our first granddaughter, Halley, lies in that surreal box, and there is nothing I can do to make it better.

As a mom, I was always good at making my kids' pain go away, but I am helpless to fix this. *God, what about our bargain? I'll be good, and nothing bad will happen. What about that? Huh? Are You listening?* My heart pounds like a jackhammer. My mind commands strength and composure, but my heart yearns for an emotional tsunami. My heart wins a little as a few tears fall when I look around and see the sadness and tears of friends and family who love us and would fix it, too, if they could. I put my arm around Marla in an effort to comfort her and wish I could hold her in my lap as I did when she was little and something bad happened. That had always made it all better. Everyone begins to sing the great hymn of our faith, "Great Is Thy Faithfulness," and I feel as if angels are surrounding us, singing in beautiful, heartfelt harmony soothing our souls.

More tears slide down my face. Only God can uphold Marla's friend as she sings the soulful Chris Rice song "Come to Jesus." This stirring ballad has become one of our family's favorites. The song's last line declares the victory that comes at the end of a believer's life: *Fly to Jesus, Fly to Jesus, Fly to Jesus and live!* Our precious Halley did fly to Jesus, and now she lives!

What if your life impacted hundreds of people all over the world? What if your life strengthened the faith of others? What if your life inspired others to try harder? What if your total helplessness led others to God and prayer? What if you fulfilled God's purpose for your life? Would you not have lived a successful life? Our Halley, who couldn't move, breathe on her own, or even cry, accomplished all these things in her short fifty-five days of life. What can we accomplish in eighty or ninety *years* of life?

Halley's life inspired our family in many ways. One evening we jotted down thirty-one lessons we'd learned from her, such as God loves us through his people; words and notes of encouragement are so meaningful;

life is valuable and worthy no matter how it comes; sometimes we are totally dependent and have no control; there is time to fulfill God's purpose for our lives; everyone loves a baby; crying is good; and our fifteen-year-old son's question, "How can anyone pay to have their baby killed?"

Our suffering deepened fifteen months later when Marla gave birth to a little boy, Porter, who had the same unknown, unnamed condition Halley had. When our youngest daughter, Laura, heard the news, she summed it up by blurting out, "What is God doing?"

That's what we all wanted to know.

My husband, Mark, and I were continually amazed at Marla and Nathan's immutable love, devotion, and commitment, not only to their children, but also to each other. Nate wrote a note to Marla during some of the most difficult days telling her there is no one else in the world he would want to go through this with, and he's more committed to her than ever. Even though Nathan attended medical school and needed to be in class, he chose to be there for Marla and their baby. With the prevalence of divorce in medical school and among couples who lose a child, Marla and Nathan's commitment to their marriage and Nathan's eventual graduation is a testament to God's grace.

We proudly watched as Marla and Nathan made life-and-death decisions, handled grief, and leaned heavily on God. Their pastor told us that in all his years of ministry, he had never seen a young couple handle profound loss as well as Marla and Nate, and they were godly examples and blessings to so many. Loving Halley and Porter, telling stories about their hospital experiences, and finding joy in the small things replaced anger, bitterness, forever asking why, or resentment toward God. The most negative comment I heard Marla say was, "This really stinks." One day after getting the second death certificate in the mail, Marla remarked to Nate, "Halley and Porter are having a much better day than we are."

Our family's reactions to such intense sadness were not always positive and productive, of course, but we each worked to respond in ways that would bring glory to God. Mark frequently updated friends and family with encouraging e-mails; one son dedicated his basketball season to Halley; another wrote a theme for school about God being in control; our youngest wrote notes and spoke at her youth group; and our daughter in college visited often to support and be a friend to Marla. With the help of my sister-in-law, I created two memory scrapbooks that honor Halley's and Porter's lives.

After our hard-learned lessons, Marla and Nate adopted Shepherd from birth. He's our red-haired miracle from God, as he fits right in with his two red-haired aunts. Shepherd has many people who love him as a special gift from God. Then, last summer another wonderful gift from God arrived. Marla gave birth to Owen, born healthy—and crying! What a wonderful sound! Bringing Owen home from the hospital was one of the most exciting and emotional days of my life. I thank the Giver of life for those two boy blessings.

Remember my bargain with God? Well, I realized that God doesn't make deals like that. Unfortunately, we live in a sick world, and I'm not immune to it just because I love and serve Him. I thank God often that I grew up in a Christian home during those happy days, but I've discovered that even in the midst of great sorrow there can be great joy when we look for God's purpose in our lives.

Someday I'll find myself walking up to a big house— a mansion actually—not on a sidewalk, but down a street of gold. And there at the window of heaven will be my heavenly Father waiting for me and next to Him will be two little ones. They'll both run out to meet me, and we'll hug and cling to each other, excitedly praising God that I, too, have finally arrived home.

A NOTE FROM THE EDITORS

This original book was created by the Books and Inspirational Media Division of Guideposts, the world's leading inspirational publisher. Founded in 1945 by Dr. Norman Vincent Peale and his wife, Ruth Stafford Peale, Guideposts helps people from all walks of life achieve their maximum personal and spiritual potential. Guideposts is committed to communicating positive, faith-filled principles for people everywhere to use in successful daily living.

Our publications include award-winning magazines, such as *Guideposts, Angels on Earth,* and *Positive Thinking*, best-selling books, and outreach services that demonstrate what can happen when faith and positive thinking are applied in day-to-day life.

For more information, visit us online at www. guideposts.com, call (800) 431-2344, or write Guideposts, P.O. Box 5815, Harlan, Iowa, 51593.